Praise for *How Should a Christian Date?*

I've known Eric for a lot of years, and, as his pastor, I've walked with him through the ups and downs of his own dating experiences. His stories will make you laugh, cry, and at times, even wince. These pages are full of clear insight and practical wisdom. I hope that the lessons he's learned and the scars he's earned can become a source of wisdom and healing for you wherever you are on your journey.

GLENN PACKIAM
Associate Senior Pastor, New Life Church
Author, *Blessed Broken Given*

This is a very current, relevant, and practical look at Christian dating. Reading this book has been a great delight as Eric has written in a very open and vulnerable gritty and genuine way. There is no pretentiousness here, no judgment, or criticism, or a list of dos and don'ts! It is like having a good coach coming alongside to encourage and hopefully advise, but always with your success and very best at heart. Wisdom learned from life's experiences, not just from reading a book. Eric gives wise guidelines of how to live and love by celebrating singleness, cultivating friendships, and building good foundations and character before finding a future good mate. Becoming emotionally healthy is key to marrying out of want, not out of need.

MARK PARKER
YWAM NZ DTS training leader, teacher, elder

Eric Demeter writes passionately and practically to Christ followers who are seeking to do the "dating thing" well. He doesn't try to prescribe a template for the way to date, but rather offers helpful prompts for those wishing to pursue healthy dating relationships. If you've been around the dating block or are new to the process, I recommend you give this book a read!

SHAWN HOLTGREN
Vice President for Student Development, Bethel University

An immensely readable and practical guide for developing healthy habits in dating. Eric gives us biblically sound advice for growing ourselves, respecting others, and honoring God in a culture that says "anything goes."

LISA ANDERSON
Director of Boundless.org, author of *The Dating Manifesto*

Eric
Demeter

How Should
a Christian
Date?

It's Not as Complicated
as You Think

MOODY PUBLISHERS
CHICAGO

All Scripture quotations, unless otherwise indicated, are taken from the New American Standard Bible®, Copyright © 1960, 1962, 1963, 1968, 1971, 1972, 1973, 1975, 1977, 1995, 2020 by The Lockman Foundation. Used by permission. www.Lockman.org.

Scripture quotations marked csb have been taken from the Christian Standard Bible®, Copyright © 2017 by Holman Bible Publishers. Used by permission. Christian Standard Bible® and CSB® are federally registered trademarks of Holman Bible Publishers.

Scripture quotations marked esv are from the ESV® Bible (The Holy Bible, English Standard Version®), copyright © 2001 by Crossway, a publishing ministry of Good News Publishers. Used by permission. All rights reserved.

Scripture quotations marked niv are taken from the Holy Bible, New International Version®, NIV®. Copyright © 1973, 1978, 1984, 2011 by Biblica, Inc.™ Used by permission of Zondervan. All rights reserved worldwide. www.zondervan.com The "NIV" and "New International Version" are trademarks registered in the United States Patent and Trademark Office by Biblica, Inc.™

Scripture quotations marked nkjv are taken from the New King James Version. Copyright © 1982 by Thomas Nelson. Used by permission. All rights reserved.

Scripture quotations marked nlt are taken from the Holy Bible, New Living Translation, copyright ©1996, 2004, 2015 by Tyndale House Foundation. Used by permission of Tyndale House Publishers, a Division of Tyndale House Ministries, Carol Stream, Illinois 60188. All rights reserved.

Scripture quotations marked tlv are taken from the Tree of Life Translation of the Bible. Copyright © 2015 by the Messianic Jewish Family Bible Society.

Names and details of some stories have been changed to protect the privacy of individuals.

Some material originally appeared at ericdemeter.com.

Edited by Ginger Kolbaba
Cover design: Kelsey Fehlberg
Interior design: Ragont Design
Cover illustration of man with glasses #1 copyright © 2019 by D-sign Studio 10 / Shutterstock (1767125222). All rights reserved.
Cover illustration of man with glasses #2 copyright © 2019 by D-sign Studio 10 / Shutterstock (1759304480). All rights reserved.
Author photo credit: Sarah Wheway

Library of Congress Cataloging-in-Publication Data

Names: Demeter, Eric, author.
Title: How should a Christian date? : it's not as complicated as you think
  / Eric Demeter.
Description: Chicago : Moody Publishers, [2021] | Includes bibliographical
  references. | Summary: "God didn't mandate one way to date. Instead, He
  laid out principles for wise and healthy relationships among believers.
  Eric Demeter-a single guy who has given this subject much thought-thinks
  daters don't need artificial rules, they need wisdom about how to apply
  the relevant principles in God's Word"-- Provided by publisher.
Identifiers: LCCN 2021017854 (print) | LCCN 2021017855 (ebook) | ISBN
  9780802420848 | ISBN 9780802499196 (ebook)
Subjects: LCSH: Man-woman relationships--Religious aspects--Christianity. |
  Dating (Social customs)--Religious aspects--Christianity. | BISAC:
  RELIGION / Christian Living / Family & Relationships | RELIGION /
  Christian Living / Love & Marriage
Classification: LCC BV4597.53.M36 D46 2021 (print) | LCC BV4597.53.M36
  (ebook) | DDC 241/.6765--dc23
LC record available at https://lccn.loc.gov/2021017854
LC ebook record available at https://lccn.loc.gov/2021017855

Originally delivered by fleets of horse-drawn wagons, the affordable paperbacks from D. L. Moody's publishing house resourced the church and served everyday people. Now, after more than 125 years of publishing and ministry, Moody Publishers' mission remains the same—even if our delivery systems have changed a bit. For more information on other books (and resources) created from a biblical perspective, go to www.moodypublishers.com or write to:

Moody Publishers
820 N. LaSalle Boulevard
Chicago, IL 60610

1 3 5 7 9 10 8 6 4 2

Printed in the United States of America

Contents

Less Pain and More Joy in Dating

The one who gets wisdom loves life; the one who cherishes understanding will soon prosper.
—PROVERBS 19:8 NIV

D ozens of first dates.
Three serious relationships.

One broken engagement.

You may wonder, *Does Eric even want to be married?*

Yes—like yesterday!

I hesitated to write a Christian dating book as a single guy. Don't get me wrong, I love this topic, but it's painful to write about dating when I'm still waiting for its fulfillment in marriage. Plus, dating is controversial. In the 1990s, one unmarried guy was lauded for his bestselling dating book. Years later, many in the church wanted to see him thrown into the sea with a millstone tied around his neck for his false teachings.

At least controversies help us to think. It's better to write something worth debating, right? Who likes a bland read? Have you heard the phrase, *Better to slowly chew a steak than scarf down stale bread?* Probably not, because I made it up. This book is a well-seasoned steak, meant to be savored while it sparks your gray matter to consider: *How should a Christian date?* I'll provide plenty of answers, though it will be up to you and God to decide how you apply these principles to your situation. For example, if you're a single woman interested in a guy, is it best to wait, flirt, or flat-out share your feelings? I'll suggest women have the option of asking out men, but you'll ultimately have to choose what's right for you. Hold that grenade for later.

Writing a dating book might mark me with a target, but demurring wasn't an option. I've watched unmarried men and women wane and wander in relationships for decades, not sure of what they're doing or how they intend to get to marriage. They remind me of people in those online videos who aimlessly meander in the streets engrossed in their cellphones and suddenly smack into light poles and fall into fountains. While clips like these are hilarious, experiencing the frustration of a directionless relationship, disappointment from unmet expectations, and heartache from breakups aren't so funny.

Dating has many obstacles, but never fear, we'll work together to help you avoid them. For instance, if you won't let go of a bad relationship simply because of all the time you've invested in it, throughout these pages you'll find warnings of *Look out for the light pole!* What about people who break up but get back together only because they "miss" each other? That'll be another *Whack!*

Finding reliable information on dating is difficult. Though the Bible gives us principles to follow, it doesn't mention dating. If you attempt to mash your romance into a cookie-cutter pattern after the patriarchs and matriarchs in Scripture, here are some of the options afforded you:

- God put Adam to sleep, and he awoke to meet his wife, Eve. (Gen. 2:21–22)
- Abraham's servant found Isaac's wife at a spring in Nahor. (Gen. 24)
- Jacob was conned into working for the love of his life, Rachel, for fourteen years by her father. (Gen. 29:1–30)
- Caleb awarded his daughter, Achsah, as a wife to Othniel for conquering a city. (Josh. 15:16–17)
- God condoned Samson to pursue and marry a Philistine woman, in contradiction to His own commandment to the people of Israel. (Ex. 34:12–16; Judg. 14:1–4)
- Ruth provocatively slept at Boaz's feet so that he would marry her. (Ruth 3:1–4:12)
- Saul gave his daughter, Michal, in marriage to David only after he produced a dowry of a hundred foreskins from the Philistines. (1 Sam. 18:24–27)
- Esther was mandated to compete in a beauty pageant. King Xerxes fell in love with her, and she became queen to a kingdom that spanned from India to Ethiopia. (Est. 1:1; 2:1–18)
- God instructed Hosea to marry the perpetual prostitute, Gomer. (Hos. 1:1–3; 3:1–3)
- God confirmed Joseph should wed Mary through an angel in a dream. (Matt. 1:20–25)

It would be weird to rely on any one of these stories as a rubric for romance today. God highlighted specific marriage stories in His Word because they played an integral role in His plan for His people. Marriage was arranged in most Ancient Near Eastern and Jewish cultures and consisted of a conversation between the "groom's parents and the bride's parents."[1] India, Saudi Arabia, Israel, and Japan still practice the ancient tradition today. Can you imagine your mom and dad returning from the neighbor's house and announcing that they found you a spouse? The closest I've come to this method is letting my mom set me up on a couple of blind dates.

If the biblical examples don't work so well, what about friends and family? Their hearts are in the right place, but their relationship advice often comes with unwarranted jabs like, "What's taking you so long?" and, "Why are you making it so complicated to find a spouse?"

On Sunday mornings, it's worse. Singles become veritable dating orphans at church because many pastors sidestep the topic altogether. They fear the fallout from encouraging their members to date. The last thing pastors want is to be blamed for a broken relationship if they encouraged two people in their congregation to go out.

But like any valuable endeavor, dating is risky—potential pain is part of the process, but you needn't wander in it alone.

I'm here to help. Using the Bible, research, wisdom, and my own dating experience, I'll synthesize the best information about Christian dating in the pages ahead. We'll go on this journey together, as I give you a comprehensive, step-by-step approach to dating. Although your next boyfriend or girlfriend won't show up on the first date with an instruction manual, *How Should a Christian Date?* is as good as it gets. This book offers the best dating principles written in a fresh and humorous way without all the unhelpful additives we so often hear. As a result, the process of finding a spouse will become clearer, more fulfilling, and more fun—all as you learn to honor God with your dating life. I will expose wrong beliefs and unhealthy habits that cause *needless* heartache in dating. I hope the truckload of dating mistakes I've already made helps you experience fewer in your own life.

How Should a Christian Date? is a unique book because I have dated both as a worldly guy and as a follower of Jesus. I didn't become a Christian until the age of twenty-one, and I understand how secular and Christian dating are the same and how they are different. As a new believer, I threw myself into studying Scripture, reading books, and meeting with other guys at 6:30 a.m. to find out how to be a godly man. At the same time, I dissected my own relationships and the paths others took to marriage. The Lord also connected me with a phenomenal mentor, teacher, and father-figure, Dr. Timothy Nelson. Tim held a Ph.D. in marriage and family therapy, and we met together for sixteen years. He not only helped me heal from my insecurities and my parents' divorce but also taught me the art of Christian dating.

I came to realize that God didn't invent dating, our culture did. What I have learned from dating inside and outside the church is that there's no right way to date, just many wrong ones. A divine formula doesn't exist for how to meet a boyfriend or girlfriend, date, and get engaged. Yet the Lord doesn't leave us in limbo. He is the author of marriage, so He cares about how we get there.

The Bible gives you a framework in finding a spouse, not a formula. How you encounter your future spouse and the way you date will probably look different from your friends. Freedom and flexibility don't mean moral absolutes don't exist—they mean you need to apply God's principles within His boundaries. In following the Lord's precepts, you get to decide what works best for you, and that's what this book is about.

Minus God's boundaries, a one-size-fits-all approach doesn't exist, thus I don't espouse an ironclad approach to dating in any one way. In other words, we get a "big yard" to date within. That said, God does give single men and women a framework to follow. Following the parameters of the Bible, this book aids you in discovering what style of dating works best for you and how to create a plan through every stage of the relationship. To some, elements in this book may sound too churchy; to others, too liberal. If I can stir the pot at either extreme, I've done my job.

I also pray that by dispelling dating myths, addressing how to evaluate your relationship, and teaching you the best way to deal with a breakup, your relationships will experience more clarity and less pain. These four chapters alone will help you make wiser dating decisions. But every chapter is written with you in mind—a single man or woman who wants to learn what the Bible teaches, along with what research reveals, on relationships. Hopefully, I can also put a smile on your face as you read. After all, dating shouldn't be drudgery. As Dr. Henry Cloud states:

> Dating is not only a wonderful time of life, but also a context for enormous spiritual and personal growth. You learn so much about yourself, others, God, love, spirituality, and life through dating. Done well, it can be fulfilling in and of itself. Done well, it can be one of the most fun and rewarding aspects of your life. Done well, it can lead to a good marriage.[2]

After reading this book, you'll be able to:

- Describe the person you want to marry
- Make better and faster dating decisions
- Save yourself from unnecessary pain
- Break up well

- Bring clarity to the confusion of dating
- Know when you've found "The One"

It matters how you date. Your future marriage, your walk with Christ, and your own well-being depend on it.

CHAPTER 1

Is Marriage Better than Singleness?

There is no one path of service, but whatever a person's calling is, grace will be given so that that calling may be fulfilled.
—LEON MORRIS, *THE GOSPEL ACCORDING TO MATTHEW*

I've circled the Christian and non-Christian dating block more times than I'd like to admit. People interrogate me as to why my dating hasn't led to marriage.

"Are you looking for perfection? Is singleness your calling? Did you let that special gal get away? Did you eat lead paint chips as a kid?"

Respectively, I answer, "I don't think so. I hope not. Not sure." And, "That's a good possibility."

Inquisitions don't help. I don't know why I'm not married. As someone said, it's "wise not to ask whys." I never wanted to be a "bachelor to the rapture," and being an older husband and father wasn't part of my Jeremiah 29:11 plan.[1]

When I was younger, I always thought people who weren't married by age thirty lingered alone because they were socially diseased, like relationship lepers. Then I became one. After I was thrust into the "real world" and secured a steady job as an IT professional and bought a house, many thought it was a perfect time to find a good woman and get married. I agreed. But as the years passed and I dated, only more of my guy friends moved in. Confused outsiders began giving me that incredulous, tilted head and raised-eyebrow look, implying, *What's wrong with you? Why don't you have a wife?*

Though I found it uncomfortable to give a continual update on my love life, looking back, I didn't need to worry about when I would get married—nor did they. Because God knew His plans for me. And He still does.

The truth is, if I do get married or if I remain single, I'm okay, because both singleness and marriage are gifts from God. As one theologian put it, "God blesses one person with the call to be single, and another he calls to marriage."[2] The apostle Paul knew that "whatever you do, do all things for the glory of God." (1 Cor. 10:31). The same patriarch even made a strong case that singleness was a special option for serving Christ. Paul goes as far as saying, "I wish everyone were single, just as I am. Yet each person has a special gift from God, of one kind or another" (1 Cor. 7:7 NLT).

Whatever route you take in life, one thing I know is that if you're not content as an unmarried person, then marriage won't fulfill you. Marriage isn't superior to singleness. I didn't always think this way, though.

Dating Didn't Soothe My Loneliness

Ironically, for many years I thought marriage was better than staying single, even though I never dated during that time with any serious intention of finding a spouse. My primary goal while attending a secular university wasn't to meet my wife but to make out. Slogging from relationship to relationship, I was searching for intimacy with a woman to fill the crater-sized hole in my heart. The physical closeness temporarily soothed the loneliness, but, like a fleeting sunset, the feeling never lasted. It wasn't meant to.

Relentlessly I sought validation from the opposite sex but was never satisfied, always pursuing but never at peace. After each breakup and new love interest, I felt lonelier than I had with the previous one. I was lost.

At that time I had no clue what the Bible said about singleness, dating, and marriage, because I didn't read the Bible. I thought all Christians were zealots. Weird. Stiff. Too religious and irrelevant. In fact, I was in my third year in college before I understood the difference between the Old and New Testaments. Heavy metal, not Hillsong, boomed in my car. During summer jobs, I stamped plastics in a factory alongside ex-convicts, not evangelicals. My college life consisted of socializing, dating, and studying—probably in that order.

At one party, I stood in the corner by myself, pensively evaluating the crowd and nursing a red plastic cup filled with Jungle Juice to fit in. A terrible sinking feeling settled into my stomach. *I hate feeling alone. Where is God?* I wondered. Soon followed with, *Is a fraternity party where I want to meet my wife?* I felt devastated that life wasn't going as planned and that dating didn't fill the loneliness I felt. I clung to the idea that if I found a goddess to marry, the loneliness would cease. Before God transformed my beliefs about relationships, however, He had to change *me*.

I wasn't a complete heathen at that point. My parents' inculcation of "being a good person" and periodically attending the Roman Catholic Church kept me from making worse dating decisions at university. At one point, a family member had even taken me aside and said, "Eric, you'd be a great priest." But the watershed moment came from a sermon at an evangelical church near my hometown. The pastor said, "You must jump off the cliff of faith, give everything to God, and He will catch you." I felt like he was speaking directly to me. So moved by it, I finally decided to fully surrender my life to Christ.

Within a few months, I lost the motivation to party. God gave me a hunger for the Bible, and I attended worship nights instead of dance clubs. Rather than aimlessly pursuing women, I cut off all illicit relationships. The next spring break, instead of soaking in the sun with wild beachgoers in Florida, I raised money for my first mission trip and ministered in Haiti for a week.

I had to work hard to understand that dating and marriage don't fix loneliness, only Jesus does. Similarly, I had to come to terms with the fact that being married isn't better than remaining unmarried. It isn't that a spouse won't profoundly enhance our lives—it was God who inspired Solomon to write, "An excellent wife, who can find her? For her worth is far above jewels" (Prov. 31:10). But wives or husbands weren't meant to usurp the place of the Savior in our lives. Without Him, we have nothing; with Him, we have everything.

As a starry-eyed baby Christian, I felt like an incomplete person again. Religious culture didn't seem to agree that singleness is of equal value, often viewing it like a virus that needed to be cured. Older married churchgoers rarely went out of their way to include me in their activities after the service. However, many Christians concede that not being "tied down" is utilitarian for Christian service. In ministry settings, I've received slights like, "Since you don't have a family, Eric, can you be the one to do the shopping for the office party?"

My non-filtered self wanted to say, *Let me get this straight: Because I'm single, my schedule is clear by default, and I couldn't possibly have any other essential tasks to complete today besides driving around town buying party supplies for everyone? Seriously?* Singleness is much more valuable than being recruited for the mundane.

I also wonder how many capable and spirit-filled single men and women get passed over for leadership positions in the church because they are unmarried. Even today, I feel less respect is offered to me and my unmarried counterparts. It's wrong to think that being unmarried is just a transitional phase, or that finding a spouse means that you're mature. Getting married only means you have a wife or husband, not that you've "made it" in life.

When I did date, the primary pair of dating directives that the church chiseled into my brain were *Be intentional* and *Don't have sex before you're married*. Though profitable advice, it didn't stop there. Well-meaning men and women told me, "You'll find your wife when you focus on the Lord" or, "Run after the Lord, and eventually you'll find the right woman running right alongside you." And, one of my favorites: "You'll meet your spouse when you stop looking." I also never understood why I had to pursue a woman with laser-like focus toward marriage when we just had one date. Apparently, I wasn't finished gulping the purple Kool-Aid from my college days after all.

There Are Only Ten Commandments

If you decide to marry, it's not better than remaining single. "Thou shalt marry" is not the eleventh commandment. You are not required by God to find a spouse, and no one needs a husband or wife to live an outstanding life. According to Jesus, you'll spend eternity with God *not* being married, as marriage won't exist in heaven (see Matt. 22:30)—how's that for perspective? If you marry, your spouse will be just one of the many blessings you'll receive in the short time you have on earth.

While some people are meant to be married, some are called to stay single. Jesus said, "There are also eunuchs who made themselves eunuchs for the sake of the kingdom of heaven" (Matt. 19:12). "Eunuchs" is a physical state in some cases and also can be a metaphor for people who choose to remain single to serve God better.[3] As Professor John Nolland states, "Some people will sense the challenge to forego the possibility of marriage for the sake of the call of the kingdom of heaven."[4] Many iconic inventors, writers, and missionaries never married. A single woman named Agnes Gonxha Bojaxhiu served in Calcutta, India, for fifty years, aiding thousands of poor people. You know her as Mother Teresa, and the Catholic Church canonized her in 2016.[5] And what about others, such as the Wright Brothers, Nikola Tesla, Condoleezza Rice, Amy Carmichael, Susan B. Anthony, Octavia E. Butler, Jane Austen, or the apostle Paul? They lived purposeful, powerful, and fulfilled lives—all without a spouse. Then there was Jesus—the Prince of Peace, the Bright Morning Star, and the Alpha and the Omega—God's "only begotten Son"—He never married.

If you are single and desire to be married, you don't have to wallow in waiting for a spouse. I've taught English and Bible classes to refugees in Europe, preached the gospel in Mongolia, and discipled incarcerated teenagers in the United States. I've had the privilege of witnessing ruby-red sunsets in New Zealand, absorbing striking thousand-year-old ruins in Angkor Wat, and swimming in the azure seas of the Mediterranean. All the while, deep friendships, further education, and professional positions have strengthened my character and satisfied my soul. My single life has been anything but wasted, and many of my married friends long for the freedom I have.

Marriage is a choice, and both marriage and singleness have benefits and drawbacks. One thing I know for sure is that if you aren't happy in singleness, you won't be happy in marriage. Chloe was a kindhearted, vivacious, and intelligent woman in her late twenties. She grew up with stable Christian parents, loved Jesus, and studied fine arts at a top university on the West Coast. After college, she incessantly pined, "If I were only married to a great guy, my life would be perfect." Taking action, she joined a new singles group and met a handsome and successful gentleman who had just moved there from out of state. They courted for a year then got married. Chloe was living her dream. For a while, at least. To her surprise, she soon felt wistful. She convinced herself that if they could adopt a baby girl, then she'd be fulfilled. Months later, they were not only able to adopt one baby, but twins. Chloe was ecstatic for a while, but did she find contentment? No. After that, money became tight as her husband had to take a pay cut to keep his job. Chloe believed that if he could just land a high-paying position at a new company, then she'd be satisfied. And on and on the sickly cycle went.

Maybe you'd like to shove Chloe into a corner and not-so-gently remind her of all her blessings? From the outside, she looked as though she had it all. Yet clearly, her hopes for a "perfect life" were insatiable. She had a God-sized gap in her life that no human could fix or fill. We can find peace, joy, and contentment in the here and now only in Christ and Christ alone.

Marriage Is a Blessing, but It Isn't Superior to Singleness

If we're emotionally and spiritually healthy, it won't nullify our longings for marriage and children. Years of extended singleness—especially for those who ardently desire marriage—can be miserable. Most people want a spouse. Though data shows that marriage rates are declining, we don't know yet if this trend means that more people will ultimately opt out of marriage completely or if people will continue to marry but at an increasingly older age. Historically, the vast majority of the US population will be wed at some point in their lives whether they wed when they're younger or older.[6]

The idea of finding a spouse tugs at our heartstrings. Many of our deepest hopes and dreams are tied to marriage, like emotional intimacy, family, sex, and children.

I love my single life, but I want to be married. At home, hanging out alone and/or with my guy friends sometimes gets kind of old. I'd be just as satisfied spending slothful afternoons cuddling on the couch with my sweetie as I would be surfing in Sri Lanka.

I can't wait to have a constant companion in marriage, a beautiful sex life, and the joy of writhing in pain from stepping on a Lego my kids dropped on the carpet. I'll love walking into church with the person I can always sit with instead of playing the tiresome game of *find-a-friend-in-the-haystack*. In any case, I'll continue to thrive whether I wake up to my wife in the morning or next to a German Shepherd. There's a reason why God said, "It is not good for the man to be alone; I will make him a helper suitable for him" (Gen. 2:18).

For years research has documented the physical benefits of marriage. Couples who wed live longer, experience fewer strokes and heart attacks, and survive a major operation more often.[7] Another study found that married people are 14 percent more likely to survive a heart attack and leave the hospital two days sooner than their single counterparts.[8] As researchers noted, "The size of the health gain from marriage is remarkable. It may be as large as the benefit from giving up smoking."[9] Regarding mental health, marriage not only "reduces depressive symptoms for both men and women,"[10] but couples "have a lower chance of becoming depressed."[11] In *The Meaning of Marriage*, Dr. Timothy Keller notes that the holy union also provides a "profound 'shock absorber' that helps you navigate disappointments, illnesses, and other difficulties."[12] When life gets you down, you have a tangible shoulder to cry on. Indeed, "if either of them falls, the one will lift up his companion" (Eccl. 4:10).

And if you're a man—I hope you're reading this—researchers "found that young men in their 20s were more likely to have difficulty with depression and excessive drinking if they were single, compared with their peers who were married. Forty-eight percent of single men ages 24 to 29 reported they were frequently drunk, compared with just 28 percent of their married peers."[13] Marriage is exceptionally healthy for us guys.

And what about sex? I've heard some say it's overrated, but I'd like to engage in extensive personal research with my wife before agreeing with that conclusion. Movies shortchange us by portraying the *search* for a spouse and sex before marriage as the most exciting part of any relationship. But many experts agree that husbands and wives, not the sexually promiscuous, experience the most under-the-sheet activity. Why? Marriage provides convenience, consistency, and security. God designed a permanent relationship bond for us to feel safe and secure in our most vulnerable places. Who else would you be more comfortable sporting your birthday suit to other than the one who promised never to leave you?

Our culture might paint sex within marriage in drab colors, but true intimacy follows vows and the ceremony. Keller states, "Passion may lead you to make a wedding promise, but then that promise over the years makes the passion richer and deeper."[14] Simply put, the best part of your romance will be after the altar, not before it.

If you're a lady, the hunt for a hunk pales in comparison to the happiness, safety, security, and intimacy that a covenant union with a husband will bring. Guys, you might have the skills to woo women to date, but your most profound satisfaction will be in winning her heart daily in marriage. Committed couples get to dream together, share life's mountaintops and valleys, feed other people, and build a kingdom-life beside one another that glorifies God.

> **Marriage is a big deal, but compared to eternity, it's a mist.**

And yet we are also well aware that many must battle to keep their marriages afloat. I know that even if you find a godly man or woman to marry, at some point the relationship will be challenging. As my mentor taught me, manure might smell bad, but it makes great fertilizer. You can learn a lot about yourself, grow in your character, and even become closer to your spouse through conflict. Indeed, as the apostle Paul noted, those who marry will face certain kinds of "trouble," and he wanted to "spare you" (1 Cor. 7:28). If you take your eyes off of Christ, obligations to kids, in-laws, and the desire to please your spouse could make it harder to be fully devoted to the Lord (1 Cor. 7:32–35). Married couples also face the risk of a stale marriage, infertility, divorce, the pain of a spouse or a child becoming sick, or any number of potential tragedies unique to a husband and wife.

Caveats aside, God designed marriage to be an abundant blessing for you, your spouse, and the rest of the world. But it is not superior to singleness. And the good news is that if you get married and have problems, you can still have hope. One long-term study found that "two out of three unhappily married adults who avoided divorce or separation ended up happily married five years later."[15]

Either Way Is a Win

Both singleness and marriage have unique benefits. If your identity, happiness, well-being, and ultimate hope is rooted in marriage and not in God, you'll have a tough life. God is most interested in you knowing Him, being loved by Him, and loving others regardless of your relationship status on social media. Marriage is a big deal, but compared to eternity, it's a mist. Finding a spouse or staying unmarried is a "win-win." Either way is a vanishing mist compared to the kind of life we'll have with Christ in eternity. So go ye therefore into the world and know that there's no battle between getting married or staying single, and you're just as complete, capable, and competent as your betrothed counterparts.

CHAPTER 2

Why Is Christian Dating So Weird?

"Just say a simple, 'Yes, I will,' or 'No, I won't.' Anything beyond this is from the evil one."
—MATTHEW 5:37 NLT

My unmarried roommate Charlie was climbing into his late thirties when a woman invited him to join her at a wedding reception.

Maybe not a terrible first date? I thought. *It's a bit intense but fair enough.*

Charlie accepted and seemed to have a good time. The day after their wedding date—I mean, date-at-a-wedding—the woman appeared on our front porch with a wrapped present for Charlie.

Isn't that sweet?

He opened it to find a framed picture of them at the wedding. *Awkward!*

Don't couples wait to give printed photos of themselves until they are an actual couple? Where would you even place a photo of you and the gal from a first date? On the mantle above the fireplace? On your desk at work? In a box in the attic?

While your dating life may not include that kind of extreme experience, I'll bet you've got your own awkward dating stories. But if we're being honest, *all* dating is awkward—inside and outside the church. Here's the key: dating is awkward, but it doesn't have to be *weird*.

What's the difference? Something (or someone) is awkward when it's uncertain, ineffective, or precarious. We primarily use awkward to mean *uncomfortable* and *clumsy*.[1] Picture a newborn giraffe attempting to stand—that's awkward. Her legs are weak and shaky. She's unstable. For many newborn animals, this is a normal process. Similarly, whenever we lack skills or try something new— like dancing or playing the guitar—it's awkward. I stepped on more than one woman's toes while learning East Coast Swing Dancing— klutzy to be sure, but par for the course. Weird, on the other hand, is bizarre. If that same awkward-but-adorable giraffe was born with six legs and pink and purple spots, then it's weird. A creature like that would be completely irregular. Awkward is normal; weird is abnormal.

Imagine dating a guy or gal, breaking up, and then ending up at the same small group. It would certainly feel awkward, but it's also completely normal. Weird is when your ex shows up to the same meeting wearing a Halloween costume so you won't recognize him or her. See the difference?

Keep in mind that weird isn't always bad; it's just abnormal. It can hold elements of strangeness and excitement. The gangly green characters in movies like *Star Wars* and *Star Trek* are entertaining because they are curiously weird. People and situations can be awkward and weird at the same time—just as dating can be.

The bottom line is that awkwardness is inevitable, but weirdness is optional. Christian dating at its best means accepting the awkwardness but minimizing the weirdness.

Why Is Dating Awkward?

How could dating *not* be awkward for Christians and non-Christians alike? If you're serious about getting married, the person you're drinking organic coffee with is not just a *regular* guy or gal. If things go well, your date might become your husband or wife for fifty-plus years, your sexual partner, and the mother or father of your children. He or she will be the one taking care of you when you're old and sporting a scooter. No pressure there! Or the relationship might go the opposite direction and suddenly smack into an unseen wall and fall flat on its face.

Whatever you do on your first date, at some point you both end up staring at each other wearing the *I-wonder-if-this-will-go-anywhere?* glasses. Unanswered questions swirl around in your mind, causing anxiety. The stress makes communication like swimming through gravel. *Does he like me? Do I like her? Will he contact me to go out again? Am I attracted to him? What are the skeletons in her closet? Does she want to live in my state? Does he want to have kids?* It's difficult to remain calm in the present when your brain is in the future.

Finding a date via a website or app doesn't squash the awkwardness of the first get-together. Even after being matched online—with plenty of texting and talking on the phone—your date still may walk into the coffee shop and not look anything like he or she did on the video chat! Who *is* this person?

What about that detailed, ten-mile-long list of expectations we drag into a new relationship? Surely *that* won't make things awkward. Instead of staying curious and getting to know others for who they are, it's easy to occupy ourselves with how many traits they tick on our must-haves list.

And what about the end of the date? Saying goodbye can be uncomfortable. Should you offer a friendly wave? Should you shake hands? Opt for the full-frontal hug? Keep it safe with the Christian side hug? Or do you make up your own, like the arching cathedral hug, so you can leave plenty of room for Jesus? How will you react if your date goes all-in for a kiss goodnight?

Dating is also awkward because the process is imperfect. For some couples, it's linear: a man and woman seamlessly flow from friendship to dating to engagement to marriage. (That's probably the model couple you see in the picture frames for sale at Target.) For others, it takes years of relationship curveballs and breakups to end up with the right person.

Dating is risky. It's difficult to know how much to share when a relationship is brand-new and uncertain. The temporal nature of dating creates a conundrum. Your heart might get broken or you could break one. You must risk a certain level of self-disclosure, but no one likes to bare their soul if a relationship is on a trial basis. That's one of the toughest parts of dating—much of it is temporary. The relationship could culminate in a blissful wedding or it could crash miles before the altar. Which way will it go?

Even in established dating relationships, awkwardness endures. How will you respond if the man you're in a relationship with invites you on vacation to Florida with his parents? Does that mean it's serious? Are you ready for the intimacy this would bring in your relationship?

Embrace the Awkward

Take a deep breath. Relax. I don't want to be the Debbie Downer of Dating, because the process of finding a spouse should be fun! And if laughter is an excellent antidote for awkwardness, then dating needs to abound with it. After one hiking date, nerves got to me and I forgot I parked in front of a large, wooden railroad tie. It was eight inches tall. I confidently let out the clutch in first gear, pulled my sports sedan forward, and ran over it.

To make matters worse, my car got stuck on top of it. Looking for the nearest hole to crawl into, my face turned flush while I attempted to laugh at my *faux pas*. I didn't make eye contact for several minutes, but by the time we arrived at the froyo shop, I had recovered.

Many of us have had our Homer Simpson *D'oh!* moments as we spend time with someone new. Dating is better when we can keep it light and learn to laugh at ourselves and the awkwardness of getting to know a potential spouse. I hope everyone makes it to marriage with at least one hilarious dating story. Maybe *you've* even given a framed picture of yourself after a first date. Don't worry. This book is a no-judgment zone.

Honesty and vulnerability can also mitigate the awkwardness in dating. I arrived to meet one woman I had connected with online and asked how she was doing. "I'm nervous," she replied. Her humility and transparency broke the ice, and I offered that I felt the same way. After we both admitted our first-date jitters, we were free to chuckle about it and enjoy the date. The best daters learn how to regularly deal with their emotions and effectively share their expectations.

There's no circumventing the fact that dating is uncomfortable, no matter how hard you try to avoid it. The awkward is here to stay. Embrace it. Even in extremely uncomfortable situations, find a way to get a good laugh and go with the flow. The point is to give yourself and your dating relationships the space to experience the typical tension, questions, and discomfort. It's normal. Take dating seriously, but not too seriously.

Christians Who Take It to the Next Level

On the other hand, somehow some followers of Jesus can elevate the natural awkwardness of dating to a new level and make it weird. Have you heard a Christian use any of these expressions?

- "God told me we were going to get married."
- "God told me to break up with you."
- "The Holy Spirit didn't give me peace about you."
- "I had a dream about you and it was from the Lord."
- "God gave me this Bible verse for us."

Although spiritual assertions like these might be sincere, mediating quotes from heaven is often incredibly confusing when it pertains to dating. Even worse, they can come across as spiritual manipulation. Dating is already an imperfect process, but adding superfluous religious lingo turns it into an enigmatic one. Our faith in Christ should make relationships easier not harder, *right?*

One guy abruptly approached a woman I know and claimed, "God told me that you would be my wife." She was surprised, but told him she would pray about it. Days later, she returned and responded by saying that the Lord wasn't speaking to her in the same way about him. He became upset, left in a huff, and accused her of not hearing God correctly. It ruined their relationship.

There is no one right way to choose a spouse, but there are

many wrong ones. Touting that "God spoke to me" then getting angry that the other person doesn't see it the same way is a wrong one. This man's immature rebuttal only proved that he wasn't ready to be with her anyway, because mature Christians are honest, open, and humble when they make mistakes. Maybe he could have won her heart by honoring her no, backing off, and humbly accepting her answer. If he felt the same way a few months later, he could have contacted her again and been direct: "I know you said you weren't interested, and I'm sorry for how I acted. I really like you. I think we'd be great together. Has anything changed with you since we talked before? Or do you still see us only as friends?" No fluff, no room for ambiguity. If she said no a second time, then he could drop it altogether.

I'm not here to thwart how God wants to speak into your dating life, but I'd recommend waiting to share anything related to "God told me about you" until later in the relationship. You might scare off a viable mate. If you insist on staying prophetic, be open to being wrong, and immediately follow up your assertion with questions like, "What do you think?," "How do you see it?," and "Would you mind praying about this?" By showing humility, you'll not only protect your reputation but honor your beloved's ability to hear God's voice.

> God regularly allows unexpected twists and turns in relationships to grow you to be more like Him.

It's easy to outrun reality when we want something (or someone) so badly. In romance, feelings can cause fuzziness in our spiritual antennas. The combination of sexual attraction, excitement, and fear often jumble the signal. Understanding how God is communicating to you in romance is indispensable, but tread lightly and give it time. And apply His revelations to how He wants to guide *your* decision process, not someone else's, in dating. If you question how God is speaking to you and prompting you to act, ask others.

Of course, I'd be ecstatic to receive a booming voice from heaven on whom to marry. The truth is, visions, dreams, or spiritual liver-quivers aren't needed to kick-start a godly relationship, and the lack of a sign from heaven doesn't need to keep you from exploring a relationship with another Christian. Some believers are willing to let their lives pass them by as they needlessly wait for a sign on whom to ask out on a date. Stay open to the more mundane ways God might want to bring you and your future spouse together. Whether meeting in college, through a club, at church, through friends, or on the internet—every way God brings people together is holy.

It would be easy to write off spiritual experiences in dating as anomalies. But as I researched for this book, I was surprised to learn how many men and women experienced signs, dreams, and visions from God that specifically revealed who they would (or wouldn't) marry. Heidi Baker, the famous missionary and cofounder of Iris Global, was praying at a church in Mexico City when God gave her the first and last name of the man she was going to marry. Roland and Heidi Baker wed six months later and have been happily married for four decades.[2]

But just because God *can* write the name of your spouse across the sky, He probably won't. He regularly allows unexpected twists and turns in relationships to grow you to be more like Him. The process of what you learn in dating is as important as the outcome. For example, being open, vulnerable, and sharing your feelings when you're interested in someone is awkward, but, at the same time, a necessary stepping-stone to Christlikeness and emotional maturity. Furthermore, the normal ups and downs of dating allow you to grow in courage, display wisdom, and learn to hear His voice in a way that a one-off divine intervention wouldn't.

If everything in relationships were easy, you'd never be stretched and learn about yourself and other people. I couldn't have written this book without having made a bevy of mistakes myself. Even Heidi Baker—as often as she hears directly from God—was engaged to another man before she met her husband.

What about Dreams and Visions?

My friend was deployed with the marines overseas when he received an odd email. The message was from a woman he hadn't seen since his college days. They had dated before he moved across the country to start a new job after graduating. In the message, she described the dream she had about him in vivid detail and how she believed God was bringing them back together as a couple. Then she asked if he believed her dream was true.

His first thought was a profound, *Uh . . . I have no idea. We haven't seen each other in years.*

What could have been an easy I-like-you email transformed into one that was slightly bizarre and confusing. Did she expect him to have his own dream about her?

Some say that dreams, revelations, and visions are still viable methods through which God communicates to us today. Others claim that these methods ended after the early church. While the theological disagreements will no doubt continue, we can't deny how God miraculously matched men and women together in the Bible. For example, Abraham sent his servant to find a wife for Isaac and told him that the Lord "will send His angel ahead of you, and you will take a wife for my son from there" (Gen. 24:7). Similarly, the

Bible outright says that "this was of the Lord" that Samson married the Philistine woman (Judg. 14:4). Joseph, Jesus' earthly father, also heard from God in a dream: "Do not be afraid to take Mary as your wife" (Matt. 1:20). But we need to be extremely careful in trying to copy how God worked in these cases. These were all ancient Israelites called out to play exceptional roles in unfolding God's plan for salvation and ushering in the Messiah. And for every one of these incredible stories in the Bible, we have millions of other people who were never mentioned in Scripture who followed their culture and allowed their parents to set them up.

Spiritual revelations are fantastic and essential for our faith—in all their forms. Because love is complicated enough, don't rush to share them. Here's a good rule of thumb: save the nightly aberrations until you have made a serious commitment in the relationship. Again, revelations like this will be fun and exciting to tell your *fiancé*, not your potential boyfriend or girlfriend. Before there's a serious commitment, it's only confusing. Later as you and that cute guy or gal head toward marriage, sharing how God is speaking to you about the relationship will be encouraging to the other person. You might be surprised to discover that God confirmed you to them as well. Timing and your motivation are the primary keys to consider.

My friend's wife did it the best way. The Lord gave her dreams about him before they were married. At first, she didn't want to date him, but God kept reminding her about him for several nights. Eventually, without telling him of how the Lord was working in her, she followed God's lead and went out with him. Surprisingly, their first date went horribly. But they continued dating, and she fell in love with him. A year later, they were married, and have a loving, God-centered family today. She was wise, and she didn't tell him about the dreams until they were well into an established relationship.

Fleeces and Cows

Like the donkey that spoke to Balaam in Numbers 22, one guy I met believed God answered him through an animal. Only a month before his wedding, he had angst about marrying his fiancée. As he waited at an intersection in his pickup truck, he noticed a cow in a field across the street. He locked eyes with the bovine and watched as it slowly shook its head from left to right. This man interpreted this as God saying no to his marriage, and he canceled the wedding. I promise that I didn't make this up.

It's clear this guy was having second (and third) thoughts about his marriage *before* he asked for a signal from above. It's easy to see what we want to see when our hearts are already leaning in a specific direction. I'm not here to judge how God chooses to settle your internal dispute, only to offer you the necessary caveats when seeking divine intervention. Maybe it was God who initiated the cow-confirmation. Maybe the animal was shooing away an annoying fly from his face. In any case, he made the right decision. Years later, he happily married another lady and today has four beautiful children.

Gideon might have tested God's voice with a fleece, but be careful with signs. When you ask for a rainbow, you might get one. Or you might get a farm animal. Many times you won't get a heavenly confirmation at all. A lack of divine intervention doesn't mean you should or shouldn't be in a relationship. When making serious dating and marriage decisions, there are better indicators to consider, like listening to the wisdom of your friends and family, assessing the health of your relationship, and measuring your own desire to be with that person. If you do receive a heavenly harbinger, present it to a trusted community for scrutiny. Keep in mind the sign is for *your* faith and confirmation, not to be shared with the other person until after you commit.

Again, it's not that these spiritual mediations can't be true, but we avoid saying them at the beginning or end of a relationship simply because they are *not helpful* in dating. For example, the next single woman you ask out doesn't need to hear that *God* wants you to date her. She needs to know that *you* want to date her. Likewise, the guy you're dating probably won't respond well to you saying "God told you" to break up with him. Out of respect, he needs to hear the relationship is not something *you* want. It's scary, but some men and women who say, "God told me to marry you," say, "God told me to divorce you," years later.

The Lord doesn't need you to mediate His voice for a relationship to succeed. Your responsibility is to stay close to Him throughout the entire dating process. In dating well, everything is based upon a strong relationship with Christ, and the best way to portray what He's doing in your heart is by having the courage and integrity to speak with clear and unambiguous language. Instead of saying, "God gave me a dream about you," simply ask, "Would you like to go on a date?" What about expressing an "I like you" instead of "I have peace about dating you"? You can never go wrong with being straightforward. Even replying with an "I don't know" or "I need to think about it" is also perfectly respectable and honest.

We must be especially keen to rid ourselves of spiritual superfluousness when breaking up with someone.

If someone says, "You're a great Christian guy, but God told me no," we'd think there was more to the story and that they weren't telling the truth—and we'd be right. When we say that God is saying no, *we* are the ones who mean no. Christian dating is about honoring others, and we do this with clear language. Jesus doesn't mince words when He says, "Let what you say be simply 'Yes' or 'No'; anything more than this comes from evil" (Matt. 5:37 ESV).

Why Do We Do This?

By speaking prophecies in the beginning, middle, or end of a relationship, we only add another layer of complexity to already tricky
conversations. Remember when I said there's no one right way to
date, just many wrong ones? Spouting Christian mumbo jumbo is
a wrong way. Christian philosopher Dallas Willard nailed it when
he said, "Some people want to have God's distinct instructions so
they will not have to be responsible for their actions."[3] If we give
ourselves a gut check, we *use God* when we utter Christianese.
Jesus becomes our hook to catch a date and our escape hatch to
bail us out from a relationship. We wish that God would do our
dirty work. Rather than facing our fear of rejection or of hurting
someone, we spiritualize our language. Our hearts might be in the
right place as we yearn to cushion a breakup or avoid a second date.
We attempt to "stay friends" by saying "God told me," or "It's not
you, it's me." But God isn't our scapegoat—even if He put a certain
man or woman on our heart to date, it's always *our* choice (and
theirs) to start or end a relationship.

It's uncomfortable and scary being honest, but we are always
safest when we speak the truth in love. Most people respond best to
straightforward and concise language. Wouldn't you rather hear an
authentic no from someone in the form of "I don't see this going to
marriage" instead of "I'm just looking for friends right now"? A kind
but direct answer might sting, but it will save everyone involved
needless suffering later. You can trust that whether a friendship is
saved or not, you can leave the outcome to God.

Besides confusing the relationship, using unnecessary spiritual language muzzles our maturing process. Sanctification is
the Christian term for becoming like Christ in all we say and do.
Paul charges Timothy, "If anyone cleanses himself from what is

dishonorable, he will be a vessel for honorable use, set apart as holy, useful to the master of the house, ready for every good work" (2 Tim. 2:21 ESV). Though Paul was warning about empty speech and false teaching in the context of the church, the universal principle can also apply in our romantic relationships. So facing our fears is often the doorway to maturity and growing Christlikeness. My mentor, Dr. Tim, taught me always to go toward the *USA* stuff in life—whatever is *Uncomfortable, Scary,* and *Awkward.* God only wants you to fear Him (see Luke 12:4-6). When you face your fears and do something good you'd rather not do, you're growing in faith and fealty to Christ. You can speak clearly because you trust God with the outcome. As you move toward USA conversations and become more direct, your self-esteem, joy, and dating confidence will increase.

The best dating is fueled by the courage to say what is ultimately right and just without deliberately sidestepping the awkwardness. And we can season our words with gentleness and kindness. Resolve to use lucid language, put away pleasing people, and serve an audience of One.

Stay Awkward, but Let God Be Weird

Dating is often fraught with residue from past hurts, poor communication, and unspoken expectations. Cryptic communication makes it worse. I took five courses of Japanese in college, but I don't think it was as confusing as learning to speak Christianese.

Love, on the other hand, is transparent and honest. There's no spiritual arm-twisting when we love. Playing the God-card in asking someone out or breaking up is weak at best and manipulative at worst. Show how close you are to the Lord with your *actions*, not your words. Your faith in Christ is displayed much more through respecting physical boundaries, speaking clearly and courageously, and showing gentleness and grace if a person wants to end a relationship with you.

At the same time, be sure to give yourself space and grace to have klutzy dating moments. Mistakes are unavoidable and perfect language is impossible. Go with the flow and laugh it off if you speak something spiritually whacky. Our goal isn't to get a master's degree in dating—it's to find a husband or wife. Consider this: if dating isn't awkward sometimes, you might be a professional dater. And if you're a professional dater, you need to stop reading this book and get married. Seriously, do you want to get to the point where you're so suave in relationships that you don't occasionally bumble over your words or drive over a railroad tie?

It's important to remember that weird isn't inherently bad; it's just fantastical. God seemed to fuel some relationships that developed in strange ways in the Bible. When Ruth laid at the feet of Boaz in Ruth 3, it was odd (and highly provocative). When God commanded Hosea to marry a prostitute, it was bizarre. We trust that God knew what was best, and His will was accomplished in these specific cases. I don't understand why He chose these strange means, but God does what He wants. He's God. For the rest of us, *please-oh-please* stop using weird and overly-spiritual phrases. Can we leave the weird stuff to the Lord? Doing so will give you freedom to grow in Christ and in your relationship with another.

Thank goodness God still works in the midst of our dating blunders. Remember my friend Charlie at the beginning who received the picture frame after the first date? That eyebrow-raising gift didn't stop him. He asked her for another date, and they were married a year later. Go, awkward dating!

CHAPTER 3

"Scalpel, Please." Dissecting the Word *Date*

We keep moving forward, opening up new doors and doing new things, because we're curious . . . and curiosity keeps leading us down new paths.

—WALT DISNEY (QUOTED IN *MEET THE ROBINSONS* CREDITS)

Have you ever repeatedly spent time with someone and assumed you were dating? Neither of you mustered enough courage to initiate a DTR (Define the Relationship), but then you discovered they asked someone else on a "date." Your heart hit the floor, and you said to yourself, "Weren't *we* dating?" But they only saw your time together as "hanging out." If singles let a four-letter word slip out, it's from frustration over the term *dating*. The turmoil stems from the fact that there is no consensus for *what* a date is, let alone *when* it happens. Ask five different Christians for the definition of "dating" and you'll get five different answers.

Labeling an activity as a "date" isn't a cure-all, either. Has someone ever asked you out and you later realized that person was also dating others simultaneously? You thought you were the lone person in their heart, but they explain it's normal to get to know more than one person at a time.

We need a common understanding and foundation for what dating is. So let's look at some definitions and specific language to make our dating smoother and our communication clearer, which can help us decide more quickly whether to begin a relationship or move to the next person.

What Is a Date?

As we've mentioned before, there is no one right way to date, just many wrong ones. One wrong way is to misunderstand what a date is and why we're doing it. We waste time and send mixed signals to others when we date for any reason other than searching for a husband or wife.

Be at ease—in no way, shape, or form am I suggesting you need to know you want to marry someone before going out with them. Please don't saunter into your next internet date with a ring tucked in your fifth pocket. There's a big difference between blurting, "I'm considering marrying you," after the second cup of coffee and tacitly allowing the goal of finding a match to motivate your selection process. But the premise of dating is spending time with someone because you're curious about the *possibility* of marrying them at some point.

Scheduling time with that attractive man or woman only because you don't want to be alone Friday night doesn't qualify as a valid date. Neither does a romantic stroll in the park with Sam or Sally when you've already surmised that this person is a no for marriage. Dating for any reason other than a chance for marriage will confuse the person, waste time, and entangle your heart in a DOA (Dead on Arrival) relationship. Dating needs to be fun but also have a purpose—just "hanging out" isn't it. In all likelihood, you won't know you want to marry them before going out, but that's the whole point of dating—to find out. So go on a date if you hold even an inkling of interest that this man or woman could be your spouse someday. However, if you already know they aren't the one, then save your energy, time, and money.

There's no doubt God uses dating for reasons other than marriage. According to Henry Cloud and John Townsend, "Dating gives people a context to meet and spend time with a wide variety of people. They can find out what they like, what they need, and what is good for them."[1] In most cases, it will probably take multiple dates with

> **We waste time and send mixed signals to others when we date for any reason other than searching for a husband or wife.**

different people to clarify the type of person you're looking for. But the primary purpose of dating isn't self-discovery.

Likewise, another side benefit to dating is that it exposes weak character traits and provides a context for each person to mature. I know my romantic relationships have made me a better man. I've learned to be vulnerable, communicate more clearly, and develop a robust prayer life. Four agonizing breakups taught me how to be honest with my heart while moving through a relationship slowly. But benefits like feeling close to someone, experiencing personal growth, and distilling the kind of man or woman you want to marry are ancillary. Dating is ultimately meant to get you to marriage—certainly not a place that's a lab for your lapses or a playground for your passions. The key is understanding that dating well is about holding the tension between the goal of marriage while enjoying the process of finding out if that will occur.

Gray Areas of Interest

Dating can be easy when your motives and feelings are black and white. You fall head over heels for someone, date, form an exclusive relationship, get engaged, and marry—all without unnecessary drama. Some couples are clear from the start that they want to be with each other and bypass that painful cycle of breaking up and getting back together again.

But what if it isn't black and white, but more gray? Perhaps you're like me, and the process has been filled with ambiguous and ambivalent feelings. Your heart is cloudy about someone, or you have feelings for two people at the same time. What are you to do when the romantic path isn't clear?

Take Liv, for example. Liv met Greyson two years ago at a party. Whenever they run into each other at social gatherings, they always exchange pleasantries and enjoy small talk. But Liv has never thought of Greyson as anything more than an acquaintance who is a nice guy. Recently, however, he began attending her Bible study, and she has started to appreciate his sense of humor and kindness toward others.

After one gathering, he asks her, "May I take you on a date?"

Liv is curious but only feels an ounce of physical attraction toward him. Should she give Greyson a chance? If she is willing to explore a possible relationship with Greyson that could eventually coalesce in marriage, then absolutely. But if there's a subzero chance she and Greyson could never be more than friends, then no. Otherwise, I'd recommend that she go on a couple of dates with Greyson to reveal where her heart is.

In another case, George has known Cindy for more than ten years. They've talked at length and even played on the same softball team. She's an attractive lady with an unwavering faith, but George has never seriously considered asking her out. "Cindy and I are *only* good friends," he insists with a chuckle.

Lately, however, he's taken special notice of her. He begins admiring her positive attitude and work ethic. *Should I ask her on a date?* he wonders. He must answer two underlying questions: (1) Is he willing to risk his friendship with Cindy to explore a romantic relationship? (2) In his eyes, is she marriage potential? If he answers both with yes or "I'd like to find out," then a date—or several dates—is the way to do that.

Your romantic path will become clearer as you gain information, and information can only be gained by taking a risk and going out on dates. Dating is the precise context you need to answer the most important questions you have about a potential life partner. Otherwise—more often than not—close guy-girl friendships turn into a web of confusion.

Keep Out of "Friendlationships"

Whatever you decide, stay out of "friendlationships" (or flirtationships): those complicated, semi-romantic, undefined, friends-with-emotional-benefits relationships that leave people hurt and confused when an actual relationship doesn't develop. These quasi-couples experience some of the benefits of a genuine committed relationship, such as texting every day, spending quality time together, and connecting through emotional intimacy.

But in reality, these friendlationships are pseudo-relationships that neither party has defined. Whatever the euphemism, if you tell your friends that you and this person are "just friends," and they say, "yeah, right," you're probably in a friendlationship.

Consider Sal and Jenny. Sal kept asking his neighbor Jenny to join him for grocery shopping on Saturday mornings. To Sal, Jenny was never on his radar for marriage or even a date. Picking out his peanut butter Cap'n Crunch next to this attractive woman was just a way for him to spend time with a charming friend, share some laughs, and complain about his actual dating life without any obligations or fear of judgment.

After several weeks, however, Sal began to feel a new attraction to her. Unsure of his next move, he waited to broach the topic. Jenny, on the other hand, had been interested in him romantically for more than a year, and if he asked her out, she would have dated him in a heartbeat. To Jenny, it was never about the shopping; it was about spending time with Sal, hoping that he would ask her out. Unfortunately, they got caught in a friendlationship.

Sensing that Sal didn't feel the same way, Jenny began ignoring his daily messages and canceling their Saturday-morning Safeway rendezvous. She put up healthy boundaries, which left Sal hurt and confused. He wisely used this time away from Jenny to assess his feelings for her. He realized he missed her and, in fact, discovered that he did like her. After a couple weeks, Sal confessed his interest and asked Jenny out. They dated for a year, got engaged, and wed four months later.

Not all friendlationships have happy endings, though. Hanging out without dating often ends in heartache, because exclusivity breeds intimacy. The more time you spend with someone, the more attached your heart becomes. Friendlationships are a dilemma—a catch-22. They live in the netherworld between friendship and romance. But setting boundaries on platonic relationships will make room for the romantic kind. Jenny did that with Sal, and it not only protected her heart, it also forced Sal to take a good, hard look at his interactions with her and decide what he truly wanted.

When Sal openly shared his feelings with Jenny, he initiated a DTR. These conversations eliminate the cloudiness in relationships by diagnosing their current status along with offering a prognosis for the future. Specifically, they are heart-to-heart discussions to decide the relationship's status. They answer the questions, "What are we?" and "Where are we going?" Done early, they break ambiguity, protect hearts, and set the course for how two people will move forward. These conversations are exciting when both people want the same thing, as in Sal and Jenny's case, but they will be painful if one person desires to move toward romance and the other doesn't. Even if you dread DTRs, they are inevitable, so better to do it sooner than later.

DTRs can be invoked by either party. If Jenny shared her feelings for Sal first, that wouldn't mean she was asking him out. She would only be gaining information to make decisions for herself and her future.

If you aren't sure if you're in a dating relationship or a friendlationship, here's my advice: if you're spending time with the person and it looks like dating, smells like dating, and your friends keep nagging you to fess up, then you're probably in a friendlationship. But don't mind-read. If your heart *needs* the DTR, then don't wait for the other person to initiate it. Have that important conversation and share where you stand. How long should you wait to figure it out? There's no rush to say anything, but listen to your emotions. When your curiosity and excitement become tainted with anxiety, frustration, or a fear that you could really be hurt if they don't feel the same way, then that is your heart's way of telling you it's time for a DTR.

Hard Starts versus Soft Starts

We've reviewed what not to do, but how *do* you ask someone out? You can approach it as a hard start or a soft start.

I barely knew the administrator at my dentist's office, but she was friendly, pretty, and carried a beaming smile. After one visit, with butterflies in my stomach, I approached her desk and simply asked, "You seem like a great woman. Would you like to go on a date?" Here I practiced the hard-start approach. With the same warm grin, she responded, "I'm sorry, I can't. I have a boyfriend. But thanks so much for asking." In the next couple of minutes, she was exceedingly appreciative of my candor and boldness. My curiosity about a potential relationship was satisfied, she felt admired, and no harm was done. Skip the excessive drama. Asking someone out can be easy.

This is an example of a hard start: explicitly asking someone for a date using the word *date*. Hard starts are straightforward, bold, and eliminate ambiguity. This approach rarely leaves room for confusion (at least in North America). The benefit to my directness with the office worker was that I received an answer immediately. She also felt appreciated for being asked, and no unnecessary drama ensued. Being candid is vulnerable—fortunately, most people realize this. Even if she says no, you'll earn her respect. Without plans for Friday night, I still walked out of the office with my head held high.

What if you're on the other end of the asking? Sometimes men and women need to consider their answers. "I don't know," "Let me think about it," and "I need to pray and see where my heart is" are all valid responses. If you need time to deliberate about a date, make sure you communicate your answer to the person who asked. If you decline, thank the person for thinking of you. If you're unsure, remind yourself that you're not deciding to marry them right now, only that you're curious to find out if it could be a possibility someday. Again, if you don't hold the slightest inkling, spark, or "what-if" in your heart, then don't go.

Unlike a hard start, a soft start is a date without saying it's one. Soft starts are implicit, indirect dates that are useful in specific scenarios, such as:

- "I'm having a few people over this weekend to watch a documentary—want to join?"
- "Are you busy Saturday? I'm hosting a game night. Are you interested in coming?"
- "Joel and I are going to the zoo Sunday afternoon. Would you and your roommate want to join us?"

Soft-start dates still hold to our definition of a date—any time you arrange with someone for discerning the possibility of marriage. Moreover, they are not a crutch, a plan B, or an easy way out when you can't marshal enough courage to ask someone using a hard start.

Instead, soft starts offer another tool for singles to use when it's unwise or untimely to ask for a date directly. As we've seen from the examples above, they can come in the form of group dates or one-on-one dates, with the latter being infested with far more pitfalls to navigate. A guy might choose a soft start if he fears an avalanche of expectations from his religious community through using the word *date*. Or if a man doesn't want a Bible hurled at him and be excommunicated from their social circle if they lose interest in a woman after taking her out a few times. In addition, some people I met equated asking a woman on a "date" with wanting to have sex. In that case, a soft start is definitely the way to go.

Can Women Make the First Move?

In most situations, I believe the man should be the one to ask out the woman. First, because Adam is the protagonist in Genesis 2 and, subsequently, the one who initiates the leaving-the-home part.[2] Likewise, Proverbs 18:22 is about the man "finding" a wife. Indeed, she is a "treasure" *to be found* (18:22 NLT). In addition, the majority of mature men won't need a woman's help to do the asking part. Having said that, however, I've known Christian guys who probably wouldn't have married their wives if the women hadn't made the first move. As we've mentioned before, there is much diversity in dating and God gives us a big yard to date within.

First, Scripture reveals the kind of man or woman to seek, but it doesn't specify who does the asking out. Remember that Ruth made the first move with Boaz. Second, initiating with a guy or sharing how you feel is *not* the same as pursuing him. Initiating means that once, or a few times, you invite him on a soft-start date with only you or in a group. Or it could be that you are the first one to break the ice and schedule a DTR. Think of initiating as trying to spark a relationship to catch fire with a few flicks of the lighter. If it does, then let the guy be the one to add fuel to it. Pursuing, on the other hand, is rolling your thumb over the spark wheel so many times that it turns black and blue.

Pursuing will turn a man away; initiating won't.

Several years ago, I received a call from an acquaintance asking if I'd like to join her on a five-hour bus trip to visit mutual friends. I didn't know her well, but we'd had flirtatious interactions in the past. When she contacted me, I was excited, and thoughts of a possible relationship swarmed my mind. I agreed, and we met a few days later.

During the ride, we spent hours asking each other questions, sharing stories, and enjoying each other's company. But she never mentioned that our time was a date, nor did I ask her if it was. We spent a couple more times together over the next few weeks.

Were those dates? I think so. Did they need to be called dates? No. Even if her intention was only to spend time together as friends, it was my job to understand what was going on inside my heart. As I pondered if there could be more for us, I ultimately decided she wasn't the one for me.

Where some churchgoers believe it's uncouth for a woman to suggest an activity with a man, a soft start empowers her to take charge of her love life while protecting her reputation. When I didn't take action and schedule an outing, my friend stopped inviting me to other exclusive events. Her soft start initiative helped us both.

Some women feel restrained by religious culture and powerless to take action, but I'm here to empower you to take a chance. Besides, isn't trying and failing better than never getting an answer? There's absolutely nothing unfeminine, improper, or unbiblical about a woman taking initiative with a guy. It doesn't mean you're brazen or desperate. It means you want to be married—and that's admirable. I have yet to meet a man who minded if a woman made her feelings known. We think it's flattering.

Staunch opponents argue that if the man doesn't lead at the beginning, he won't become a leader in marriage. Instead, of course, he will stay passive and transform into a sloth, sitting on his plush recliner all day eating potato chips and watching hours of ESPN while his wife teaches the Bible to their children. Who does the initial asking out has nothing to do with spiritual leadership, as defined in Ephesians 5:21–25.

A woman leading once or twice by sharing her feelings or initiating a date doesn't mean she must stay in that role. You can make your interest known by inviting him to a dinner party, starting a conversation with him after small group, or asking him to join you for a walk through the local arts festival. Be creative. If you've made your interest evident, and he hasn't responded, then move on to a guy who gets it. Most of the quality men you're looking for will notice your signs. And you probably won't need to ask him out explicitly. Therefore, if a guy doesn't pick up the reins and start pursuing after you've tried to connect with him, let him go.

Finally, remember the goal is to be married, not to follow a fairy-tale model of dating. Think about this: fifty years from now, when you and your husband are sitting in your rockers, playing Bingo, and eating dinner at four o'clock, will it matter who broke the ice in the relationship?

If you're convicted to wait for the man to instigate, then that's your prerogative. My only point is that it takes the same faith and courage to wait as it does to make the first move. It's ultimately up to you to discern how the Spirit is leading. Soft starts empower a woman to express her interest in a man while respecting her theological convictions.

Soft-Start Caveats

For all their benefits, soft-start dates also have their fair share of caveats for both genders. It's important to check your motivation for using one. Is it best for the situation, or are you avoiding the word *date* out of fear of rejection? If so, I urge you to be brave and "be strong" as Paul encouraged the men of Corinth to be (1 Cor. 16:13). I believe men need to be direct. Getting a no doesn't feel good at the time, but you can stand up straight with your shoulders back and be proud of yourself for trying. If you are scared to ask someone out directly, take your time, uncover the root of your fear, and allow

God to strengthen your identity before you go for romance.

The second warning is that by not using the word *date*, you might still be clueless if someone is romantically interested. Just because someone agrees to spend the afternoon with you on a picturesque drive or accompanies you to an amusement park doesn't mean he or she wants anything more than friendship. This happened to me several years ago when I invited a woman to join me for the day at a nearby theme park. I began with the soft start, because I wasn't sure if I was romantically interested in her. But after our date, I knew I wanted another, so I came clean. A few days later, thinking she understood our time together had been a soft start, I decided to be direct. I gushed, "I like you. Would you like to go on a date?" She was caught off guard and had only joined me for the company, the roller coasters, and the cotton candy.

The third caution is that if you initiate a soft start, be ready to be 100-percent honest if they ask for clarification. If she says, "Is this a date?" Smile and say, "Yes, it is. Still want to go?"

One guy I know was the king of soft starts and often invited women out for lunch after church. They'd always call him on it and ask, "Why are you asking me?" His response was, "To build a friendship with you." Fail. At that time, he needed to come clean and say, "Because I like you and want to explore a possible relationship with you."

The final and most salient warning is that you should use soft-start dating only for a short time. Though germane, soft starts are untenable. If you've initiated several soft-start activities and after a few weeks still haven't offered a DTR—or at least transitioned to the word *date*—then you are missing the point of a soft start. You need to be clear with what you are intending.

Both hard-start and soft-start dates hold strengths and weaknesses. The latter comes with a far lengthier warning label. Yet, for all their headaches, I believe we need the freedom to go on some dates without naming them every time. You must determine how much your heart can handle without having a DTR. Be honest with your motives—if you're not at least slightly considering someone as your future spouse, then spending one-on-one time, hard start or soft start, can needlessly break hearts.

Nonexclusive versus Exclusive Dating

Another dicey issue in romance is exclusive and nonexclusive dating. Exclusive dating is dating "single file." In this method, you get to know only one person at a time until you break up or until it finalizes in marriage. In nonexclusive dating, however, you get to know different people simultaneously. You might bowl with Fred on Friday and eat dinner with Frank on Sunday. But nonexclusive dating is not having three boyfriends or girlfriends at the same time. It's going on a few dates with different people to see if you desire to form a relationship with one of them. If you're dating the same three people for six months, you're not picking up what I'm throwing down. You also might be on the road to polygamy or polyandry, which are illegal in most countries.

Nonexclusive dating enables you to meet a wide range of people within a short amount of time. Online dating, speed dating, and group dating are nonexclusive. If you are interested in different people, consider going out on at least one date with each of them. (First, make sure they're not good friends or part of the same Bible study, or you might have thrown yourself into the lion's den.)

My friend Marvin took nonexclusive dating to the extreme and planned three dates with three different women on the same afternoon. To be fair, he was attempting to make his one-day trip to a different city more efficient. Unfortunately, he scuttled his hat trick when he texted the wrong gal after his first rendezvous. *Oops.* That many back-to-back dates on the same day is probably too many.

The primary benefit of exclusive dating, however, is that your heart and mind are focused on one person. It's easier to go deeper with one person than it is to divide your time between multiple people. My main problem with meeting people online was that my heart always felt split when interacting with multiple women. Other singles don't feel this way.

You'll have to decide for yourself whether you will date exclusively or nonexclusively. Listen to your conscience and to how God designed you. If you haven't had much dating experience, are young, or have recently endured a grueling breakup, then try nonexclusive dating for a while. Even if others can date different people at the same time, it doesn't mean your heart was designed for it. One woman I know understands that her heart wasn't meant for nonexclusive dating. Recently, a guy asked her out, and she made it clear that he would need to cut off all the other women he was dating before asking her out.

Like soft starts, nonexclusive dating comes with a trove of yellow cautionary lights. Be upfront and clear if you ask someone out while seeing others at the same time. They'd want to know.

CHAPTER 4

Busting Twelve Christian Dating Myths

Facts do not cease to exist because they are ignored.
—ALDOUS HUXLEY

When we were kids, my friends and I built ramps out of scrap wood to launch our BMX bikes over. We'd never play it safe and put the launchpad on grass. No, it had to be on the sidewalk or the streets, because that's what the pros did. After one painful crash, shards of asphalt embedded themselves in my knee. Before bandaging my wounds, I knew I first had to dig out those foreign objects so my knee would heal properly.

Likewise, you will date better, save yourself pain, find healing, and might even find your spouse sooner when you remove the debris that has infected Christian dating. Namely, I'm talking about myths. I already pulled out some big pebbles in the last chapter by defining dating, but there's more healing to be done. Over the years, as I've spoken with singles, I've been stunned by some of the misconceptions people believe. In fact, I created a survey and asked people to give me the most common beliefs they've embraced or heard about Christian dating. While the list was exceptionally long, I found twelve that showed up repeatedly. So it's time to bust them (in no particular order) and give ourselves the freedom to date.

Myth #1: Men Are Only Interested in a Woman's Looks

Some women blame men's superficiality for why they're still single. But it takes much more than a dazzling profile photo to land a quality Christian guy. Mature men, like women, are looking for a complete package in a spouse. We seek a woman who has a deep faith in God, a sharp mind, a servant's heart, a fun-loving personality, and that feeling of *chemistry*. For men, chemistry is the mysterious combination of a woman's inner and outer beauty that draws him to her. The truth is, a woman's looks are just one factor of many that make her desirable. She doesn't have to be a model on 99 percent of guys' nonnegotiable lists.

Of course, some superficial guys are guilty of only chasing external beauty. Women wouldn't want to give a first date to a gawking knucklehead like this anyway. (Many women perpetuate this lie themselves. They endlessly evaluate their own looks, and constantly compare their social media pictures to other women.) Especially as guys mature, questions like, "How does she handle stress?," "Does she encourage me?," "Does she have a serving heart?," and "What kind of mom will she be?" become the salient concerns.

The apostle Peter's words are timeless: "Don't be concerned about the outward beauty of fancy hairstyles, expensive jewelry, or beautiful clothes. You should clothe yourselves instead with the beauty that comes from within, the unfading beauty of a gentle and quiet spirit, which is so precious to God" (1 Peter 3:3–4 NLT). There's no doubt an outwardly gorgeous woman can turn a Christian man's head, but only a godly woman can turn his heart.

Myth #2: Getting Married Means that You're Mature

Marriage is a concentrated relationship where you get to grow up. It has been called a "crucible" for our character, because a good marriage will force you to learn how to communicate, resolve conflict, and share what's going on inside. Yet it's a myth that single men and women can't cultivate the same character through relationships with roommates, mentors, counselors, and close community. Marriage is not the litmus test for maturity any more than remaining unmarried measures immaturity. Immature men and women marry each other all the time. I've seen married couples quibble like children after being together for decades.

Maturity can be better measured by how individuals handle their emotions. Maturity is being able to feel an uncomfortable feeling while not acting upon it. How you respond to an angry co-worker, what you do when you're tempted to sexually sin, and how you follow that impulse to buy that extravagant outfit or eighty-five-inch television—these situations reveal how emotionally grown up you are—not whether you have a husband or wife.

Myth #3: If You Do All the Right Things, God Will Bring You a Spouse

For many years I thought that if I doggedly prayed, read the Bible, and staved off sexual immorality, then *voila!* I would find a godly wife. But as I write this book, I'm still waiting to be married. Now I see my future wife as a blessing from God, not as a reward for my spiritual efforts. God doesn't owe us anything. We have a grace-based relationship with Him, not a merit-based one. And whether we stay single or find a spouse, nothing can surpass the gift He gave through His Son, Jesus: "For God so loved the world, that He gave His only Son" (John 3:16).

God is not the means to an end—He is our end. He's the goal. What we are promised this side of heaven is an intimate relationship with the Father through His Son, Jesus Christ. But I see men and women, jaded in their faith, shake their fists at God and cry, "I've done everything right, God! Where is my spouse? I'll take to marrying someone outside the church if I have to!" Sure, you can do "right things" to find a mate. You can work on your character, get in shape, and update your wardrobe. You can try online dating, join a new meet-up group, or ask friends to set you up. But any attempt to decode God's combination that unlocks a husband or wife through good works, purity, or preparation is futile.

Myth #4: You're too Picky

As much as I am for getting you out there to date, I am more interested in helping you keep your standards high. Singles often hear "you're too picky" if they don't date frequently or if they turn down a seemingly viable match. But it isn't a matter of being finicky; it's a matter of holding high expectations. Famous marriage researcher

Dr. John Gottman stated that "people who have higher standards and higher expectations for their marriage (including romantic ones) have the best marriages, not the worst."[1] But if you aim low, you'll experience a lower quality relationship. Like a self-fulfilling prophecy, people who hold higher standards for marriage will find more satisfying ones. So it's healthy to stack your nonnegotiable list and wait for the man or woman who completes it. Just make sure they align with the ones that God values. Favor the traits that make for a great relationship and will stand the test of time.

Myth #5: Dating Will Solve Your Loneliness

Although dating will undoubtedly add a friend to your life, if you're extraordinarily lonely or depressed now, a boyfriend, girlfriend, or spouse won't fill that hole. Loneliness isn't caused as much by a lack of a romantic partner as it is by your need for deep and meaningful relationships now. You can find these through family, friends, and a caring church community. Wait to start a relationship until you're emotionally ready. Feelings of isolation can lead you to lower your expectations and choose to be with someone your healthy self would have avoided.

Here's an exercise: Hold out your hand and make the shape of a cup with it. Your well-being is the cup. Jesus fills it with Himself while your community tops it off. A date adds to the overflow. If you aren't full of love from God and those around you now, a boyfriend or girlfriend will never be enough.

Loneliness, as a single person, can be painful. But I've heard from marriage counselors that being lonely when you're married is much worse than when you're single. When you're healthy and single, you naturally accept that part of you that longs for the intimacy and deep companionship a godly marriage will bring. On the other hand, a lonely marriage feels magnitudes worse, because the one person you're expecting to be there for you and your emotional world isn't.

If you're single and need a friend, I'm thankful that "God places the lonely in families" (Ps. 68:6 NLT). You may not be close to your blood relatives, but your "family" could be a group of close friends, a small group from church, or an older married couple who "adopts" you in your single season.

Myth #6: You Must Know What You Want Before Going on a Date

My friend took a woman out on several dates. They had a good time together, but he sensed a hesitation in her about continuing dating. After asking her about it, she responded, "I'm still figuring out whether I'm attracted to you or not." Fortunately, he was secure in his self-image, and her response didn't sting. What was clear was that she needed time to see if they had any spark between them. A few weeks later, she got the information she needed and didn't see them moving beyond friendship. They stopped dating and amicably parted ways. Kudos to her for going out and taking a risk when she was unsure.

Dating is a process of discovery, and you don't have to have all the answers at the outset to purposefully get to know someone. What you learn will propel you to move forward or take a step back.

Myth #7: All the Good Ones Are Already Taken

The lie that asserts all the "good ones" are taken sets singles up to be stressed out and make poor choices in dating. Some university students fall into the trap of the *senior scramble* during their last year in college. Or they make their mantra, *Get a ring by spring*. On one hand, college can be a perfect place to meet your wife or husband. There are few periods in life where you'll be surrounded by so many singles. But if your search is motivated by a fear of missing out, or you're way past college age and live with regret that God left you behind, then first you have a theological problem. Heaven doesn't run on a shoestring budget. The Lord isn't scratching His head wondering if He has the right puzzle pieces to put your love life together. He loves you and only wants the best person for you. Passing in front of Moses, God said of Himself, "The LORD, the LORD God, compassionate and merciful, slow to anger, and abounding in faithfulness and truth" (Exod. 34:6). Be assured: plenty of male and female fish are still in the sea.

Myth #8: You'll Meet Your Spouse
When You Stop Looking

People offer this pithy maxim when, in their opinion, someone they know is putting too much effort into getting married. Or, if you believe the previous myth, maybe you've thrown in the towel on your search for a spouse. There is merit in not acting out of desperation and benefit in taking a hiatus from seeking a spouse. But the idea of completely sticking your head in the sand and expecting to find a serious relationship is an oxymoron. Much of what we long for, such as discovering a satisfying vocation, experiencing God, and meeting our future spouse, are byproducts of God's grace plus our labor.

The truth is, God wants to partner with you in your search. Putting energy toward dating doesn't need to include undue stress. You don't work despite God; He empowers you. Only with God can you come up with creative dating ideas and think outside the box.

Myth #9: When You Find the One, the Relationship Won't Be Work

Once you meet the man or woman of your dreams, the work doesn't end. As author, reformer, and presidential advisor Booker T. Washington wrote, "Nothing ever comes to one, that is worth having, except as the result of hard work."[2] This is true in all realms of life, including developing terrific dating relationships and healthy marriages. Any good and godly endeavor requires regular practice.

Think of the grit needed to be a Super Bowl-winning team. Professional football teams spend countless, dedicated hours at the gym and endure many sweaty practices during the regular season. They fully expect their hard work and discipline to pay off. If the team wins the championship, we'd expect the players to use words like *teamwork, endurance, sacrifice,* and *preparation* in postgame celebratory interviews.

Unlike pro athletes, who are extremely conscious of the effort it takes to win, torrid emotions for a new boyfriend or girlfriend can blind daters to the work a healthy relationship needs. The best and most satisfying marriages are the result of much sweat equity. Developing clear communication, being able to effectively solve conflicts, and learning to live alongside another person through the ups and downs of life takes time, energy, and determination.

The investment to work out your differences in a marriage isn't the same as in dating, however. Some men and women who are courting are terrible for each other. They slog through a dating relationship, taking the *It takes work* attitude to the extreme. Your best dating will take some work, but not copious amounts—too much, and it's a red flag.

Myth #10: More Dating Choices
Will Make You Satisfied

With the internet, a sea of singles awaits you. Choosing whom you marry by going out with different people is what dating is all about. But too many choices limit your satisfaction level. Scientific research on choice shows that the more options you have, the less satisfied you will be with whatever (or whomever) you pick. Consider this breakthrough study where researchers rotated two sets of gourmet jams at a grocery store. The first display had twenty-four varieties and the second display, six. Customers could sample the jams, and everyone who approached the table received a one-dollar-off coupon. Even though the table that had more varieties of jams attracted more visitors, the customers who engaged the table with fewer jams were ten times more likely to buy the jam, indicating they were more satisfied with their choice.[3]

The popular notion is that the "more choice, the better—that the human ability to manage, and the human desire for, choice is unlimited."[4] And yet other studies that included different varieties of jeans, chocolates, and other goods have all confirmed the fallacy that more choice will make you happier. We weren't designed to have endless options.

Likewise, infinite possibilities won't necessarily make you more satisfied when choosing a mate. Although it might be attractive at first, too many choices can hinder your dating and leave you feeling less satisfied. So be encouraged if you have limited romantic opportunities. Maybe you live in a small town, can't travel, or want to stay in a tight community. Don't fret, because marrying someone out of a smaller pool of singles can lead to a more gratifying relationship because you actually had less choice.

Myth #11: There's No Hope for the Homely

If you have average looks or a reserved personality, don't let that concern you. Everyone has a chance to find a date and get married. Just as you don't need a bigger pool of potential mates, singles don't need movie-star looks or charisma to find the right match.

You might roll your eyes at the statement, *It's what's on the inside that counts*. But that gooey Hallmark Channel cliché is actually backed up with research. Psychologists explain that there is a difference between your general "mate value" and "unique appeal." Dr. Paul Eastwick and Lucy Hunt "offer evidence . . . that in most romantic contexts your unique appeal is more important than your mate value."[5] Mate value is the level of someone's positive first impression, likability, and overall curb appeal. Specifically, mate value is measured by "attractiveness, charisma, or success." People who have high mate value "generally inspire swooning"[6] and get more dates.

> Making romantic decisions based on your emotions and without God's guidance is like driving a sports car two hundred miles per hour without a steering wheel.

But that isn't the end of the story. As we've already seen in the previous myth, having more choices doesn't make you happier. Second, according to Eastwick's and Hunt's research, unique value contains the attributes that make someone special, like their musical skills, aptitude to quote Shakespeare, love for classic films, or ability to listen and ask thoughtful questions. The scientists discovered that, in the long run, the specific makeup of these characteristics became far more important than the glitzy ones. As the scientists studied college students who got to know each other over three months, they found that "uniqueness dominated consensus for all desirable qualities: attractiveness, vitality, warmth, potential for success and even the ability to provide a satisfying romantic relationship."[7] The key to remember with someone's unique value is that it takes more time to unearth, because it isn't as flashy as their mate value.

If, by the world's standards, you have lower mate value, take heart. Over time, your unique value will shine brighter than mate value. Focus on being the best "you" in Christ and be proud that you're a *Trekky*, don electric hair colors, play the ukulele, or adore chinchillas. There's someone else out there who will appreciate your specialness.

If you're the person with high mate value, you might be blessed with a gregarious personality and striking looks, but be careful not to get overwhelmed by choice. There's nothing inherently wrong with going out with a lot of people—like my friend who met more than a hundred different women before marrying the woman of his dreams. The problem with cycling through so many options too quickly is that you won't get to see your date's unique value. In other words, without going deeper, you'll miss what matters most. It's better to go on more consecutive dates with the same person and give each person more time to show their best traits. As John and Julie Gottman note, "This is why it's important to consider getting to know someone slowly and perhaps go on five second or third dates rather than fifteen first dates."[8]

Myth #12: Follow Your Heart

When people say, "Just follow your heart," they usually mean "follow your feelings." As we've seen, obeying your feelings without considering other factors in a decision-making process is a sign of immaturity. It's also dangerous. Making romantic decisions based on your emotions and without God's guidance is like driving a sports car two hundred miles per hour without a steering wheel. Your mind and the Holy Spirit were designed to guide you—your feelings can sit in back.

But God *does* want you to follow your heart. Just not in the sense that popular culture teaches. When God speaks of the heart of a man or woman, it's much bigger than sentiment. The heart includes the whole person—your brain, emotions, soul, and the Spirit working within you. As Professor Dallas Willard noted, the heart is the "executive center" for believers. It is the place "where decisions and choices are made for the whole person. That is its function."[9]

As another theologian puts it, the heart is "essentially the whole man, with all his attributes, physical, intellectual and psychological, of which the Hebrew thought and spoke, and the heart was conceived of as the governing centre for all of these."[10] The heart is where you *will* things to be. To "love the Lord your God with all your heart" means that you are choosing to completely love Him with your entire self (Mark 12:30).

This is why Proverbs says to "watch over your heart with all diligence, for from it flow the springs of life" (4:23). Guarding your heart is about recognizing who you really want to let in and who to keep out. So, yes, absolutely follow your heart in dating. But that actually means combining your desires with God's guidance along with wisdom and logic to make romantic decisions.

Myth Runners-Up

There are so many additional myths in dating, it would take a whole book to cover them. These runners-up nearly made the list: *You need to be perfect before you get married; God will end your relation-ship if it isn't right; If you want them to like you, play hard to get;* and *Now that I've had premarital sex, my sex life in marriage is ruined.* Think about the myths you've carried into your dating life. Why have you held onto them? Maybe it's time to let them go and move forward into the truth.

CHAPTER 5

A 4,000-Pound Paper Weight: A Sturdy Frame Supports Dating

"Therefore, everyone who hears these words of Mine, and acts on them, will be like a wise man who built his house on the rock."
—MATTHEW 7:24

Several years ago, I had an idea about how to earn some fast cash. Since four-wheel-drive vehicles—like Jeeps and SUVs—sell for a premium in Colorado, I thought I'd buy one in the Midwest, drive it home, and sell it for a profit. A day into my search, I discovered a sporty pickup with low mileage and a five-speed manual transmission. On the outside, the cardinal-red paint was impeccable. The 3.0 liter, V6 engine was pristine and ran like silk. Underneath, however, corrosion and rust plagued the kick panels and frame.

No big deal, I thought. *A little wear and tear won't hurt.*

But I was wrong. I handed over the cash, signed the title, and drove a wobbly truck home. Upon further inspection, my mechanics dropped a bombshell: "The frame is irreparable." *Irreparable?* They were right. Rust had eaten through the truck's foundation, and it was unfixable. I had bought a lemon. The vehicle was a four-thousand-pound paper weight—useless—and my business plan a bust. I had planned to drive it one thousand miles, but it wasn't safe to drive one block. The only option left was for me to return the vehicle and incur a $600 loss.

For dating—or for any relationship—to be in good shape, it needs to be built on a solid foundation.

Inspect Your Frame

For our foundation to be solid, that foundation needs to be Christ. We prepare for dating by developing a sturdy and rust-free relationship with Him. Though the timing of the relationship we long for might be out of our control, it's always up to us how close we get to God.

Check your spiritual frame. There's no limit to how far you can run with God during your single years. Spouses make horrible saviors, so settle now who is the Lord of your life. The greatest gift you can give your boyfriend, girlfriend, or spouse is your relationship with Christ. God says of Himself, "You shall not worship any other god, because the Lord, whose name is Jealous, is a jealous God" (Ex. 34:14). He doesn't want to share His throne with anything or anyone—including your future husband or wife. Untold relationship problems form when people infuse unrealistic expectations in a boyfriend or girlfriend that only God was meant to fulfill in their lives.

Who is your ultimate security and stability? Is it the guy with the bloated bank account? Doesn't the apostle Paul proclaim, "My God will supply all your needs according to His riches in glory in Christ Jesus" (Phil. 4:19)? Who gives you your confidence and identity? Is it the hottest person you land a date with or your Father in heaven? Nothing compares to being part of God's family: "You are no longer a slave, but a son; and if a son, then an heir through God" (Gal. 4:7).

The richest, best looking, or even holiest spouses will never take the place of your Father in heaven. Only He fills your deepest needs, "for He has satisfied the thirsty soul, and He has filled the hungry soul with what is good" (Ps. 107:9). Who else but God promises, "I will never leave you nor forsake you" (Heb. 13:5 ESV)? Who else "comforts us in all our affliction" and will "bind up the brokenhearted" (2 Cor. 1:4; Isa. 61:1)?

If you're running on spiritual fumes, however, the tendency will be to usurp your well-being from another person. As relationship expert Gary Thomas notes, "Desperation and dating are a toxic mix."[1] Several years ago, I dated a woman when my God-tank was on "E." Without knowing it, I started taking my self-worth from her. Sensing my neediness, she pulled away and put up an emotional wall. My life felt empty, and I was unknowingly sucking the life out of her. I felt embarrassed when she confronted me about it, but I needed to hear how I was expecting too much from her.

> **The greatest gift you can give your boyfriend, girlfriend, or spouse is your relationship with Christ.**

Instead, "be filled with the Spirit" so you'll be able to give to that perfect person when you meet them (Eph. 5:18). To mix a metaphor, don't act as a spiritual vacuum cleaner like I did. You can't love someone unless you have experienced the love of God. As the apostle John reminds us, "We love, because He first loved us" (1 John 4:19). I needed to return to the Source of love. Jesus said, "If anyone is thirsty, let him come to Me and drink. The one who believes in Me, as the Scripture said, 'From his innermost being will flow rivers of living water'" (John 7:37–38). As my mentor taught me: God fills our cup; people add to it.

Following the Lord doesn't mean you won't feel the sting of lonely Friday nights or the angst of showing up to a wedding without a date. But jettison the notion that anyone but God completes you. Jesus has taken care of your most pressing problem—being separated from the Father: "But now in Christ Jesus you who once were far away have been brought near by the blood of Christ" (Eph. 2:13 NIV). And Psalm 18:1–2 proclaims: "I love You, LORD, my strength. The LORD is my rock and my fortress and my savior, my God, my rock, in whom I take refuge; my shield and the horn of my salvation, my stronghold."

Some men and women bounce from relationship to relationship, not knowing that they are actually yearning for God. And there's a big difference between wanting to be married and *needing* to be. If you're in an especially needy season, as I was, wait to date. Otherwise, you'll end up trying to siphon your significance from a man or woman like a Hoover or a Dyson.

Fortify Your Foundation in Christ

Successful dating and a healthy marriage will not only require an identity secure in Christ but solid character as well. Consider the courage, humility, and patience needed when you're tempted to mirror the surly attitude of your spouse on a bad day. Martin

Luther saw marriage as a "school for character."[2] The everyday ups and downs of life is one thing, but how many relationship disasters like infidelity, addiction, intractable conflict, or divorce are caused by underdeveloped character? Surely at least some of these travesties could be avoided if people carve out time every day to let God make them more like Him.

What about misfortunes you can't control? Nothing but your relationship with God and galvanized character will keep you faithful if your spouse cannot engage sexually, needs bedside care, becomes disabled, or dies at a young age. My mentor Tim was fond of saying, "It's not *if* marriage will be hard, but *when*." So why wait until you wed to smooth the rough areas in your character?

Focus now on becoming a disciple of Jesus. According to Dallas Willard, a disciple is a person "who is with Jesus learning how to be more like him."[3] Scripture says, "The one who says that he remains in Him ought, himself also, walk just as He walked" (1 John 2:6). Willard notes that this is about "learning from Jesus to live my life as he would live my life if he were I."[4] Discipleship is asking yourself, *If Jesus lived my life today, what would that look like?*[5]

Disciples are literally "learners."[6] They grow in character through practicing spiritual disciplines. Spiritual disciplines are the tried-and-true pathways to God that fortify our spiritual foundation. These include prayer, fasting, Scripture memorization, silence, solitude, simplicity, and service. Henry Nouwen stated, "Whereas discipline without discipleship leads to rigid formalism, discipleship without discipline ends in sentimental romanticism."[7] Maybe you don't hear music, snap your fingers, and salsa dance at the word *disciplines*, but you needn't be scared of them. Think of them as practices. They are pathways to experiencing God and His grace in your life.

How do spiritual disciplines help in your dating life? Consider fasting. I heard it said that you aren't really fasting when you give up food, because you are "feasting on God." By saying no to your appetite, you gain self-control. You'll realize that as you forgo lunch to focus on Jesus, you'll grow your ability to shun other temptations in dating. At some point, your body will cry out to be physically intimate with your boyfriend or girlfriend, and you'll need more than at-the-moment willpower to avoid crossing God's boundaries. Fasting gives you the grace to honor God with your body, even when it wants to go further. By forgoing the urge to eat, you'll also gain practical skills, like controlling your tongue and allowing people to speak without interrupting. How better to spend a lunch, the entire day, or three days than in a holy banquet? Who's hungry for God?

Concerning prayer, I wish I would have prayed more about who to date and dated less. I believe that in my time with God, I would have been led out of dead-end relationships sooner and saved myself (and my partner) unneeded heartache. Oswald Chambers has been attributed with saying, "We pray when there's nothing else we can do, but God wants us to pray before we do anything at all." Don't worry about what exactly to say to God—praying isn't a formula. Just start. Paul tells us, "Pray about everything. Tell God what you need, and thank him for all he has done" (Phil. 4:6 NLT).

Similarly, reading the Bible is not only indispensable in learning how to act like Christ but also shows you the kind of person to marry:

> Now for this very reason also, applying all diligence, in your faith supply moral excellence, and in your moral excellence, knowledge, and in your knowledge, self-control, and in your

self-control, perseverance, and in your perseverance, godliness, and in your godliness, brotherly kindness, and in your brotherly kindness, love. For if these qualities are yours and are increasing, they do not make you useless nor unproductive in the true knowledge of our Lord Jesus Christ. (2 Peter 1:5–8)

Need direction? Memorize Proverbs 3:3–5: "Do not let kindness and truth leave you; bind them around your neck, write them on the tablet of your heart. So you will find favor and a good reputation in the sight of God and man. Trust in the LORD with all your heart and do not lean on your own understanding."

Looking for power to overcome temptation? Burn 2 Timothy 1:7 in your brain: "For God has not given us a spirit of fear and timidity, but of power, love, and self-discipline" (NLT).

If you're having trouble forgiving someone you dated, start that process by practicing the words of Ephesians 4:32: "Be kind to one another, compassionate, forgiving each other, just as God in Christ also has forgiven you." Forgiveness is often an arduous process, and reading the Bible won't necessarily take away the pain, but it will put your heart in the right place to begin healing. I write all sorts of formative Bible verses on note cards and carry them in my pocket.

Anything you regularly practice to grow closer to God and to put on His character can be a spiritual discipline: frugality, tithing, meditating, serving, or getting involved in your community.

Regarding community, we all need to belong to a tight-knit group who both loves and challenges us. An authentic Christian community is a cohort of men and women united as Christ followers and committed to being vulnerable, honest, and encouraging to one another. Jilt the notion, *It's just me and Jesus*. More potent than memorizing Scripture by yourself is doing it with others. Likewise, fasting might feel arduous alone, but what if you recruited one or two friends to join you?

Two other pathways in my own spiritual maturity came through receiving counseling and mentoring others. Professional Christian therapy can work wonders. Like an apple covered in soft spots, many of us carry wounded areas that are sensitive to the touch. They stem from sources like divorce, dysfunctional families, loss of a loved one, or verbal or physical abuse. Left unhealed, they can fuel addictions, lies, and character flaws that hinder healthy dating. To protect myself from repeating the pain of my parents' divorce, I believed a lie that I needed to find a perfect mate. The psychology behind this wounded thinking is that if I found the ideal person, I would avoid divorce and be spared from reliving the trauma of my parents' separation. A potential spouse became my healer instead of God.

Through much prayer, counseling, and grace, God renewed my mind. I'm thankful that the man who mentored me was also a licensed marriage and family therapist and gave me seventeen years of free counseling (we called it "mentoring," but we both knew what it was). I joked with Dr. Tim that if I were to pay him, I'd owe him at least $10,000 in fees for the hundreds of hours he spent with me.

Past or present trauma that hasn't been addressed can form addictions. They seep into our lives in the forms of pornography, drugs, or alcohol but also can include social media, food, shopping, video games, and many other things. Excessive and unfettered use of social media has been linked to higher levels of depression, loneliness, and riskier decision-making.[8] Anything we become dependent upon to soothe the pain in our souls can become an addiction. Pornography is also a secret sin for many that melts a healthy mindset of sexuality into a sinful goo of unrealistic fantasies. The toxicity of porn cannot be taken lightly. Its use is associated with higher rates of anxiety and depression, erectile dysfunction, and divorce.[9]

If you can't afford a therapist or want to talk in a less formal setting, find a mature older friend or pastor to mentor you. Most ministers completed short-term counseling classes in seminary and are equipped to deal with a wide range of issues. In addition, many churches have recovery groups or host outside ones. See what format works for you. Proverbs states, "Where there is no counsel, the people fall; but in the multitude of counselors there is safety" (11:14 NKJV). Informal or formal, I believe everyone should engage in some form of counseling before they get married.

The Benefits of Concrete Character and Dating

As you grow in Christlikeness, your lens will change on the type of person to date. Have you noticed how emotionally healthy men and women end up marrying each other? On the other hand, selfish and divisive singles, gossipers, and those who throw temper tantrums will also find their long-lost twin. Constantly maturing Christians will naturally weed out dates with weak character before making a long-term commitment, thus saving themselves unneeded pain. As Proverbs 11:3 says, "The integrity of the upright guides them, but the unfaithful are destroyed by their duplicity" (NIV).

Practicing spiritual disciplines and getting help from others to heal will build concrete Christlike character within you. You'll be able to live guilt-free and with a clear conscience in your dating life. What's better than a mind at peace? For example, if you're tempted to end a dating relationship, your weaker self might have "played dead" or ghosted your partner by suddenly not returning messages and phone calls. But as you practice and embody the godly traits of integrity, honor, and courage, you'll have the ability to pick up the phone and break up in an honoring and respectful manner. Though showing integrity won't make the fear of confrontation disappear, at least you can look yourself in the mirror without guilt. Steely character will also empower you to resist sexual sin. What else but self-control, undergirded by God's grace, will empower you from going too far with your boyfriend or girlfriend and from experiencing shame and regret?

Becoming like Jesus will also make your relationships more satisfying. How? For one, you won't put pressure on your boyfriend or girlfriend to be God for you. Besides, you'll be so filled with Christ that you'll love them when they act finicky, fall short of meeting your needs, and generally act as a pain to your backside. If that's not enough, you will experience increased intimacy and closeness as pride and pretense diminish. Newfound boldness will give you courage to be vulnerable in your relationship. You'll also be in a better position to invest in the relationship and the other person and watch as both of you grow and flourish.

Likewise, the perseverance and tenacity you develop will help you weather relationship storms and even thrive in them. Jesus said that the Father "sends rain on the righteous and the unrighteous" (Matt. 5:45). Character doesn't protect you from one-hundred-mile-per-hour winds in life but teaches you to sail through them. The time you spend with Jesus, becoming like Him, will keep your ship afloat when marriage gets tumultuous. As Timothy Keller states, "Marriage is glorious but hard. It's a burning joy and strength, and yet it is also blood, sweat, and tears, humbling defeats and exhausting victories. No marriage I know more than a few weeks old could be described as a fairy tale come true."[10] Even the happiest of Christian relationships will encounter cloudy skies and high winds at some point.

What is your foundation like? How reliable is your character?

Which attributes are stalwart and which are sickly? Don't be afraid to take a candid look at what traits you need to work on. Rest easy as you work, because spiritual formation is not a pass-or-fail test—it takes a lifetime to know God and become like His Son. I'm thankful that the Lord is gentle with our spiritual formation: "Can't you see that his kindness is intended to turn you from your sin?" (Rom. 2:4 NLT). Likewise, the Spirit doesn't grab us by the earlobe, drag us to our messy closet, and leave us to clean up our character alone. God does the changing. He works with us through His grace to do what we cannot through our power alone. As 2 Peter 1:3 tells us, "His divine power has granted to us everything pertaining to life and godliness, through the true knowledge of Him who called us by His own glory and excellence."

As it's been said, "Be the person you want to be with." Become the kind of person you'd like to spend the rest of your life with. To date, be dateable first. Slip on your spiritual trainers and get to work. Marriage will be difficult at some point, so waiting until you wed to practice spiritual disciplines is too late. Start now as a single person and continue as you date. Find a routine every day to connect you to Christ that includes prayer, service, and Bible reading. Only He can solidify your spiritual frame while transforming you from the inside out. When you fall, fall forward.

Likewise, look to God for your self-worth. When your identity is in Him, you won't idolize a boyfriend or girlfriend. And your future partner will thank you for the work you do on your relationship with Jesus now.

CHAPTER 6

Follow the Stages for a Great Relationship

If you can't describe what you are doing as a process, you
don't know what you're doing.
—W. Edwards Deming

The Tour de France is the most renowned and revered cycling race in the world. For twenty-three days and over more than 2,100 miles, athletes climb mountains, whisk through valleys, endure dangerous crosswinds, and trudge through inclement weather.[1] They can whizz to speeds of over sixty miles per hour.[2] Each cyclist must complete twenty-one stages before the cutoff time to avoid being eliminated from the race. The stages offer time for riders to rest, rehydrate, fix their bikes, and prepare for the next section of the course.

Like the Tour de France, dating also has stages—not twenty-one, but five. My mentor taught me that daters don't just leap from asking someone out to exchanging rings, because there are essential steps in between. Even if you've clearly defined that you're on a date, what's after that? What is the progression from friendship to marriage? Following the stages keeps you on the same path as your partner when your relationship has progressed, digressed, or regressed. Shakespeare was right when he wrote, "The course of true love never did run smooth."[3] We need clarity; we need to take romantic relationships one step at a time.

As you move from one stage to the next, each progresses via DTRs. Think of them like five ticks that outline a relationship gauge. As you go forward, the needle clicks to the next one and stops when you get to marriage. So you start with friendship, move to nonexclusive dating, then exclusive dating, engagement, and finally marriage.

These stages allow you to take a dating relationship piecemeal while going at a slow and steady pace. By defining each stage, you'll know where you are and where the relationship is going. Following the five segments in order helps you when the romantic journey gets hazy, ambiguous, and arduous. You'll also avoid unnecessary confusion, ambiguity, and a lack of purpose in your dating. Let's take a closer look at each stage.

Stage 1: Friendship

Romance begins with friendship. The root of any friendship is enjoying another's company and sharing common interests. Think of your closest cronies. What keeps you spending time with one another? Do you revel in fashion, fine art, or the Philadelphia Flyers? Although friendship in romance will look different from hanging out with other friends now, they share a lot in common.

It's wise not to rush past developing this stage, because it sustains and enhances the other stages. When you have a bad day at work, you don't just need a boyfriend or a girlfriend to comfort you, you need a friend-friend. Friends listen, ask good questions, and pay attention when you need to vent. When you're married, you want to have sex with a spouse who is also your friend. Likewise, if you have kids and become empty nesters someday, who will you be left with? Hopefully a friend. Staying friends will increase both your chances of staying together and the satisfaction of your relationship.

As surprising as it sounds, friendship isn't a requirement for marriage. For one, in different parts of the world, singles are arranged to be married. In these cases, the couples completed the stages in *reverse* order—first comes marriage, then friendship. While each person ultimately marries for different reasons, I believe most men and women living in Western culture desire to marry their best friend. In marriage, if not guarded, kids, businesses, hobbies, ministries, and many other worthwhile endeavors could supplant the vital friendship. Have you known couples like this? They are married—but not to each other. The problem with having a central hub other than friendship is that ministries cease, businesses dry up, hobbies change, and kids fly out of the nest. Whatever different roles your spouse will be to you—lover, business associate, ministry partner, or co-parent—you first need them to be a friend.

If the man or woman you want to date is already a friend, the common context will make it easier to start. If not, you'll have to go on a date with them while developing a friendship at the same time.

Stage 2: Nonexclusive Dating (Optional)

As we've discussed previously, it's okay to get to know more than one person at the same time. While you don't want to go out with people willy-nilly, you do want to spend time praying about different people who could be great matches. If you choose this approach, know that it is smattered with a field of landmines, just like asking someone out using the soft-start dating method. Therefore, make sure they are clear on your intentions. You could say, "I think you're wonderful. Would you like to go on a date? Also—I don't want to be awkward—but I need to be honest that I'm going on dates with different people. Is that okay with you? I'm not ready to be exclusive with anyone right now. Don't worry, it's not a competition."

Give the other people the information they need to decide. If they are uncomfortable, then you can determine if it's worth letting go of all others and focusing on that one person. In any case, when you want to zoom in on one man or woman, then it's time to move into exclusive dating.

When you schedule a nonexclusive date, err on the side of a lighthearted activity. Since you're going out with multiple people, be sure not to develop a deep level of emotional intimacy. Safe dates might include going out for a casual lunch or dinner, shopping, going for a walk in the park, eating frozen yogurt, hiking a local trail, or bandying about topics you both enjoy over coffee. You can also invite them to group events. Save the rooftop candlelight rendezvous for later. Also, be wise and avoid physical affection in this stage. It is not only presumptuous but will also cloud your decision-making process.

Nonexclusive dating is always optional. If you already know you want to date a particular person, you can definitely bypass this step and move directly into exclusive dating.

Stage 3: Exclusive Dating

You reach this stage when you have squelched the "what-if's" about dating other people. Now you're focused. Whereas the friendship and nonexclusive stages may have felt as though you were swimming in muddy waters, exclusive dating is clear. It also means that you're official. At this point, you can introduce your man or woman as your "boyfriend" or "girlfriend." To have reached this stage in your relationship in a healthy manner, you must have had a DTR. You will always need to exchange verbal commitments when moving from one stage to another. If you have to ask, "Are we dating?" or "Are we a couple?" you might be in the dreaded friendlationship.

This is also the first stage that has a commitment attached to it. A protective fence guards your relationship, and you're free to get to know each other without being romantically entangled with others. There is always a gate to exit this stage, however, so don't give your heart fully to your partner. Just as this is the first stage in which you have a boyfriend or girlfriend, so it is the first stage in which you'd say, "We broke up." And just as you entered with a DTR, you'd exit with one as well.

As you keep "looking to Jesus" for your identity, security, and guidance (Heb. 12:2 ESV), you'll be building a relationship based on Him, knowing that both of you are invested in finding out if it could lead to marriage. While you keep spending time together, both intimacy and your commitment fence become higher. Your emotional and spiritual connection expands as you grow your prayer life with each other, merge friend groups, and take part in fun activities together. Because you have built a secure layer of trust, you're comfortable sharing some of your hopes and dreams, the vision for the kind of life God has called you to, and your thoughts on what a healthy family looks like.

After several months, you will perhaps begin to discuss potentially controversial topics such as gender roles, the desire for kids, and political bents. You might vacation together, kiss, or divulge a painful wound you've endured. The question of "Would we fit well together as husband and wife?" becomes increasingly salient in this stage. Also, if you have doubts about marrying the man or woman, moving to the next stage and getting engaged won't help your ambivalence. (Trust me, I know.) Take more time to find out or end it.

Stage 4: Engagement

If the relationship is healthy and you know that you want to marry this person, you buy a ring (or accept one) and get engaged. You'll be committed to marry and spend the rest of your life with this person. As you prepare, you'll likely read books about healthy marriages, undergo premarital counseling with your fiancé, share deeper wounds, plan a life together, and discuss whatever other important topics you need to address before meeting at the altar. Chapter 11 is dedicated to making sure you've found The One and know what to do after you get engaged.

Stage 5: Marriage

Most people spend the vast majority of their love lives being married, not dating. That's why marriage is not the end of romance but only the beginning. Marriage is a covenant you make with another person through God for life. Jesus said, "Therefore, what God has joined together, no person is to separate" (Mark 10:9). In marriage, you'll truly become "one flesh" as you are completely emotionally, spiritually, and physically naked with each other (Mark 10:8).

In marriage, you can share with confidence your greatest aspirations along with your deepest scars. But genuinely becoming "one" emotionally will take a lifetime of marriage. Overall, as my mentor taught me, a healthy marriage is one that feeds you, blesses others, and glorifies God. Aim for that kind.

Love Grows with Each Stage

These five stages are inherently progressions of passion, intimacy, and commitment. Robert J. Sternberg, professor of human development at Cornell University, developed a theory of love that includes passion, intimacy, and commitment: Passion is the romance, physical attraction, and erotic type of love you fully express in sex; intimacy is how connected emotionally and spiritually you feel to someone; commitment is how dedicated you are to the relationship and how devoted you are to "maintain that love."[4] In the beginning stages of dating, your level of passion, intimacy, and commitment are low, and they naturally grow higher as you move into the latter stages. For example, how close you feel to someone will be lower in friendship than it will be in the exclusive dating stage. The same holds for physical intimacy. Before you're married, holding hands, hugging, and kissing will be prevalent. In a biblical relationship, sex is celebrated to the degree that Christians have an entire erotic book of the Bible written by newlyweds.[5] At the same time, sex is intended only for a husband and wife.

Commitment precedes intimacy and passion. For example, agree to commit to exclusive dating before holding hands and spending the day together, not vice versa. Commitment is the safety net that gets stronger and can carry the weight of increased intimacy as the relationship progresses. The more committed you are, the more intimacy you can risk without fear that the other person will walk out at a moment's notice. That's what makes friendlationships so confusing and dangerous—they exhibit higher levels of intimacy without commitment.

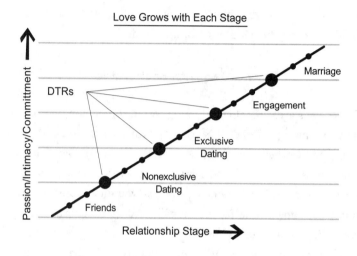

As both commitment and intimacy increase, so does the danger of heartbreak if the relationship ends. For instance, the grief you experience in a broken engagement (as I did) will be way worse than a man or woman bailing after a few nonexclusive dates. Portion out your heart slowly throughout the stages, and be especially careful about doling it out early on. Similarly, don't anachronistically leapfrog your thoughts of marriage into a further stage than what reality allows. If you've had only a few nonexclusive dates with a person you just met, then don't let your mind dwell on being engaged and act physically as though you are. If you're only friends, then think like friends, speak like friends, and act as friends. Banter about the news, shared interests, and your likes and dislikes. When you do have a DTR and begin a romantic relationship, make your conversations an accretion of lighter to more in-depth discussions over time. Talk like you're a sailboat in friendship and a submarine for the latter part of exclusive dating and engagement.

Restricting physical touch, especially in the early stages, will also help keep your intimacy level aligned with your expressed commitment. While we'll talk more about physical affection and sex in chapter 9, for now, I'll say only that nascent relationships can't handle much, if any, physical affection, because the commitment safety net is weak and won't support it.

The sooner you know that a particular man or woman is a no for marriage, the better. Your heart will thank you for not getting entangled at the serious stage if the relationship wasn't destined to go beyond a few dates. As we will discuss, the point of knowing your values, creating lists, and learning what traits you need in a spouse is to enable you to make an educated decision about a man or woman sooner and avoid unnecessary pain.

You can't avoid the possibility of being hurt, however. Sooner or later, you need to dedicate yourself to an exclusive relationship and open your heart to someone. But pray about whom to risk with—a piece of your heart is not something to give to the first babe or beau who walks by. Looking back, I was flippant in initiating some dates. I wish I would have dated less and prayed more about whom to date. Taking time, not acting on pure emotion, and talking to God before asking these women out would have given me the space I needed to see that these relationships were never destined to go beyond friendship.

Other Relationship Milestones

In addition to the five phases, you'll experience other relationship milestones, called key events. These are meaningful occasions such as holding hands, kissing, meeting someone's parents, going to church together, going on a road trip together, sharing Christmas Day with each other, changing your relationship status, and posting pictures of the two of you on social media. Like stages, these key events reflect where you are in a relationship. Think of them as smaller points occurring between the larger dots on the graph (see the graph on the next page).

The difference between stages and key events is that stages are major commitment milestones and have a fixed order, while key events are fluid and depend on each person's interpretation. Therefore, you must decide not only what you and your partner's key events are but at what stage they should occur.

Where this gets tricky—and one of the reasons I love studying relationships—is that often two people place the same key event in different stages. One person finds nothing wrong with sitting next to you at church after one nonexclusive date, but to another, doing so means you are an exclusive couple. Or suppose Pam didn't know that a key event for her boyfriend, Jim, was meeting her extended family. Pam invited Jim to her family reunion to meet her aunts, uncles, and cousins as just another fun weekend date. Jim, however, sees this same event as Pam communicating that she's ready for engagement. He'd never introduce a woman to his whole family without a serious commitment. Neither Pam nor Jim's interpretation of the same event is wrong—it only shows that they need to discuss what it means to each of them.

The stages are meant to be the driving force behind the progression of the relationship, not key events themselves. To put it another way, key events make fantastic followers but lousy leaders. For example, most would consider a kiss a key event. When that moment happens, it needs to be a *result* of a previously stated commitment, not the reason that pushed you into exclusive dating. Choose beforehand the key events associated with each stage so your feelings won't choose your stage for you. If you only want to kiss after several months of an exclusive relationship, then communicate your intention of waiting and plan on a goodbye hug until then.

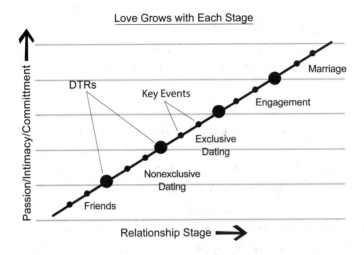

Love Grows with Each Stage

Think about some of your own key events. Again, it's best to get clear before an emotionally charged moment. What specific activities would differentiate one stage from the next in your mind? Note to yourself not just the name of the event but *why* it means what it does to you. Once your list is complete, classify each key event in one of the five stages. Step back and review your list. What you have created is a precious road map to your heart. Hold yourself accountable to this guide and use it to create healthy boundaries in the relationship. As Proverbs 25:28 states, "A person without self-control is like a city with broken-down walls" (NLT).

Now you have both stages and key events you can discuss with your boyfriend or girlfriend as these situations arise. Talking openly and honestly about discrepancies from the beginning will keep you both on the same page and stage. Being vulnerable with your key events will also grow your courage and set a healthy pattern as you continue dating.

Two quick rules: First, always move from stage to stage with a DTR. Never assume that just because you experienced a key event, it moved the relationship forward. Second, defer to the person who places a particular key event in a later stage—it's more critical and requires more commitment for them. If your partner doesn't want to share a deep childhood wound until engagement, then honor the border around it.

Step Through the Stages Sequentially

On an airline flight, my seatmate, Rick, shared how he met and married his wife. When he first met her, she blew his socks off. He burst out to her, "The guy you'll marry will be really lucky!" He asked her on a date, and they got engaged two weeks later. They have been happily married twenty-eight years. Yet Rick divulged that it took a "lot of work" for them to get to know each other after they were married. They couldn't avoid the unavoidable. In the terms you have learned, that means that they had to return and become friends, then complete the rest of the stages for the relationship to be healthy.

Building a strong foundation in the first stages will support the latter ones. That's why it's best to do the stages in order. People do skip stages, and it's not impossible to recover from bouncing around. But if you jump into an exclusive relationship with someone you barely know, for instance, you'll still need to return and develop the friendship stage.

When there's dissonance between the stage you're in now versus where your heart is, it means you haven't allowed enough time in the previous stage. Your relationship will be strained if you need to go backward. Sometimes it's almost impossible to do so. For instance, breaking an engagement and reverting to exclusive dating will not only be agonizing but improbable for the hearts involved. How many people do you know who were engaged, returned to dating, then got married? It happens, but I can count the couples I know like that on less than five fingers. Don't rush through the beginning stages. Invest early in the friendship and exclusive dating stages, and you'll have a much better chance at succeeding in the latter ones. If you jump to a further stage too soon, you might regret it. Ambivalence shows that your heart and mind weren't ready for the increased commitment. If you can, go back and work with your partner in the previous stage before moving forward again.

How Long Does Each Stage Last?

Every couple will walk through the stages at their own speed. Many relationship experts agree that it's best to date for a year before considering marriage—and I mostly agree with their assessment. Precisely how long you date is based on several factors, such as age, maturity level, season of life, and how much time you've spent in each other's presence. Inevitably, a healthy speed in dating lies somewhere between the tortoise and the hare. But you don't lose points for taking your time. Remember, the first attribute of love is patience (1 Cor. 13:4). If you don't know the person well, consider spending a month or two in the friendship stage and getting to know them in a group context first. But be diligent about not forming friendlationships.

Nonexclusive dating, which is optional, can occur for any length of time. Some people do it for years, others for only a few weeks. If your interest completely aligns to one person after only a few dates with different people, you can certainly move past this stage quickly. The fulcrum of this stage is your ability to exclusively invest in one relationship, and there's no specific timetable for that heart change to occur.

Once you commit to exclusive dating, spend at least three to four months getting to know someone's likes, dislikes, and personality while steering clear of the deep end of the emotional pool. Your relationship does have a protective fence of commitment, but there's always a gate. So risk some, but not all, of your heart in exclusive dating. I can't stress enough that you need to linger in this stage, allowing ample time to build a friendship and learn how to do life together.

> **Increased sentiment and a skyrocketing sex drive are insufficient reasons to propel you to the next stage.**

After three to six months of stable and joyful dating, be intentional in seeing if your partner meets the requirements of your nonnegotiable list.

If so, the next logical question is, "Will you marry me?" Here, you are committing to spending the rest of your life with this person. Your engagement period might be a year or a few months. It shouldn't last for more than a year or so unless you are waiting to finish college or have another extenuating circumstance. Otherwise, I'd question your sincerity. Another reason to avoid a long engagement stage is sexual temptation.

Once you make it to the final stage, that isn't the time to take it easy because you reached your "goal." Marriage is not the end of the romantic journey but only the beginning.

A Few Other Guidelines

Just as the Tour de France has rules, warnings, and recommendations, so does the process of dating. Though we've already discussed some guidelines to consider, let's look at a few more.

It's all about communication. Share regular updates with your partner at least every three months as to what stage you are in. If you and your girlfriend or boyfriend have been cruising in exclusive dating for five months, then it's time for a quick DTR. Even if you talk and the status quo remains, it's a good habit to stay honest and open with each other. Do it when you feel that five-hundred-pound anxiety-gorilla beginning to form in the room. In other words, when you need to ask, "Where are we going as a couple?" you know it's time to discuss your status again.

If you and your partner find yourselves in different stages, just as we discussed with key events, whoever is in the previous stage controls when the relationship moves forward. In other words, the less committed person has more power in the relationship. If Gary is still dating different people, but Grenadine desires to be exclusive, guess who decides when they become an official couple? Gary.

Control isn't a bad thing per se, it only means that Gary now has a power that Grenadine doesn't right now. To break any chance of an unhealthy power dynamic, Gary needs to share his heart openly with her. Equipped with this information, Grenadine can choose how long she's willing to wait for him or if it's time for her to move on.

As Dr. Tim taught me, "Lead your emotions, don't let them lead you." Increased sentiment and a skyrocketing sex drive are insufficient reasons to propel you to the next stage. When feelings commandeer the helm of your life, they'll plow over any boundaries you've tried to set. Feelings are good, but they are not God, and they're never the whole picture. Remember that you created a list of key events that supersede emotions. You need a combination of head knowledge, wisdom, advice from mentors, God's guidance, and ample time in each stage to master each one and propel you to the next.

The stages are not only designed to get you to marriage but are also meant to form you into a stronger woman or man of God. If you get married without growing in your relationship with Christ, then something in the stages went awry. Each step will challenge you to display more fruit of the Spirit, especially patience, faith-fulness, and self-control (Gal. 5:22). And just like Christ, you'll be learning to serve the other person with a sacrificial love (see Matt. 20:28).

Teach your partner these stages. Better yet, have them buy a copy of this book and read it together. In any case, he or she most likely won't know about the five steps until you share them.

Enjoy the dating process. It isn't just about continually evaluating which stage you're in or should be in. Don't forget to play. Make dates that include swinging on monkey bars at the park, competing in hilarious board games with friends, or watching a comedy flick on the big screen.

Dating needn't be a labyrinth of unmarked twists and turns. Fortunately, the five stages—friendship, nonexclusive dating (optional), exclusive dating, engagement, and marriage—can help you stay on the right path. Though following these stages won't guarantee an easy and problem-free dating experience, they will provide clear structure to help you avoid confusion. The best relationships work through each of these milestones one at a time. As you do this, you'll slowly move your emotional and physical boundaries while building trust, intimacy, and commitment in the relationship. Discuss the meaning and the stage of key relationship events. Do the stages in order, graduating to the next one after you feel secure in the one you're in.

Now let's turn to the ingredients that make a great relationship.

CHAPTER 7

Make a List but Avoid Creating Frankenstein

Do thou be wise; prefer the person before money, virtue before beauty, the mind before the body; then thou hast a wife, a friend, a companion, a second-self, one that bears an equal share with thee in all thy toils and troubles.
—WILLIAM PENN, *FRUITS OF SOLITUDE*

One mesmerizing guy my friend dated appeared to have the entire package—brains, brawn, and zeal for the Lord. For a few weeks, their relationship was bliss. They served in church together, prepared romantic meals, and kissed. Like a mummy, she'd lie in bed at night with her hands folded, pondering, *Could he be the one?*

But after several weeks a chasm arose between them. He was adamant about working a stable job and living in the suburbs near his brother's family, but she was passionate about serving the poor and marginalized in the inner city. They began frequently arguing about long-term goals. Seeking advice from friends and mentors, they tried to work it out. Finally, he confessed, "We're not compatible." Moving into the inner city was a deal-breaker for him. She wishes they would have driven their proverbial relationship car in first gear and learned each other's core values *before* speeding down the highway. Instead, they became emotionally entangled with each other and endured a gut-wrenching breakup.

Do you know what you value? Are there attributes you want in a mate that are flexible and others you'll hold onto at all costs? Have you jotted down a complete set of traits for your future spouse?

It's easy to be swept away by a tidal wave of sexual attraction after meeting a jaw-dropping person. He or she might intoxicate you with euphoria, but the critical question you need to answer is if your values match. Establishing a list of qualities in your next boyfriend or girlfriend will anchor you when you're tumbling in a whitewash of emotions. You must be careful to hold onto what God has put on your heart when a thousand butterflies in your stomach cloud your judgment. Sexual attraction and lovey-dovey feelings vacillate in long-term relationships, but your deepest hopes and dreams won't.

You will need to create two lists as you seek a spouse: *negotiables* and *nonnegotiables*. Nonnegotiables are the things you need. They are based on your most important values. You'll clutch these tighter than Marvel's supervillain Thanos grips his glove containing Infinity Stones. These items are sacred and are deal-breakers if they are absent—you'd rather let go of a person than anything on your nonnegotiable list.

Negotiables, on the other hand—though values that are still strongly desired—are flexible, nonessential, and icing on the cake.

For example, you won't compromise your dream to start a family, but you will be able to negotiate the number of kids you have. Or you'd never succumb to the temptation of dating someone outside your faith but could bend on the denomination of the church you attend as a couple. Negotiables are malleable, while nonnegotiables are ironclad.

What's on your two lists for a spouse? Do you need your partner to want kids, make you laugh, or be outdoorsy? Are living in your hometown, having strong chemistry, and exhibiting particular virtues like compassion or generosity part of your must-haves? Such questions form the criteria for why you can say yes to a date with one person but no to another. You can avoid needless power struggles and heartache while increasing the quality of your dates if you know the kind of person to run toward and the kind to run away from *before* you commit.

In hindsight, my friend was thankful that the man she dated didn't compromise his heart's desire to live in his hometown. She also avoided a lifetime of quarrels about where to live and do ministry. My mentor taught me that most fights in marriage occur because of conversations you didn't have sooner. Have them now. You can talk to yourself and God about what is important to you ahead of time.

Dating is fraught with risk, and there's no foolproof way to avoid any pain in relationships. At the same time, when used correctly, lists can mitigate the dangers of romance. The best way to make a good choice for a mate is to understand the traits God values in a spouse, but also to take into account the unique criteria and particular wiring He has given you.

Go Big on Your List

When I wrote my first list in my twenties, I included thirty-two must-haves for my future wife. Though that sounds excessive, it's nothing compared to one lady I know. She wrote several pages' worth of must-haves—a mere 106 for her future husband.

Whether your list can fit on a sticky note or requires several pages in a notebook, take a few minutes and become a student of yourself. Picture your ideal husband or wife. What foundational personality traits, distinct characteristics, and life goals would compel you to pursue a relationship with him or her?

Look at your past. What features excited you about the last person you were romantically interested in? If you are a man, what values did you see in that lady from your class that motivated you to ask her out? If you are a woman, what specifically led you to write multiple pages in your journal about that guy you met at worship night? Conversely, what values would cause you never to start a relationship or walk away from one?

> You can't build a relationship on your emotions just as you can't stay healthy eating Reese's Peanut Butter Cups for dinner.

Open your electronic notes app or grab a good old pen and paper and write down ten to twenty nonnegotiable traits you need in your spouse. Don't hold back on your list; you'll have several opportunities to modify it in the sections ahead. It's best to write your first one raw, unaided, and unfiltered. So go big, be honest, and don't over-Christianize it.

What qualities does your list contain? Did anything surprise you? How early did the word *attractive* appear in the order? Which characteristics are special to how God wired you? Did you struggle to write ten must-haves, or could you have written a hundred as my friend did? Writing down a value doesn't make it *valuable*—it only makes it important to *you*. I loved my childhood pet rock and was crestfallen when I lost it, but my rock had little real value. Similarly, people clench many things that seem pressing to them but are not to God.

Are your values valuable? Are you willing to test your nonnegotiables against what is on God's list? Will you submit this list to what research indicates make the best marriage partners? We need to be diligent to evaluate our dating criteria against misguided cultural influences, the enemy, and our sinful nature. The good news is if you value the godly traits you'll need in your own life, you'll naturally make these an archetype in whom you seek in a spouse.

Evaluating Your Attraction-o-Meter

We begin assessing your list with physical attraction, because our culture worships feelings and sexual desire. But we needn't be duped by unwise, unholy, and unhealthy standards for relationships. Passion needs to hold a place on your list, but it needn't occupy the first, second, or third spots. As my mentor taught me, when you meet that beau or beauty queen and your knees begin to shake, those feelings are like candy. Candy is enticing and oh-so-sweet, but our bodies do not function well on massive doses of sugar. God designed us to experience sexual arousal and romantic feelings. At the same time, you can't build a relationship on your emotions just as you can't stay healthy eating Reese's Peanut Butter Cups for dinner.[1] You need a substantive meal. That person's character, along with the respect you develop for them, is the lemon pepper chicken, rosemary potatoes, and arugula salad. Go for a healthy main course and trust that dessert will follow.

It's paramount to understand that long-term attraction parallels respect. Once the sugar high fades, you'll need to be drawn to *who that person is*. The more regard you develop for a person, the more beautiful he or she becomes. Give ample time for respect to develop. On a first date, some men and woman might score low on the romantic wow factor, but might their integrity, sensibility, or love for the marginalized earn them a second cup of coffee with you?

As Henry Cloud and John Townsend state, "You are initially attracted to a person's outsides, but over time you will experience his insides. His character is what you will experience long-term and be in relationship with over time."[2] I know many people who began dating their future spouse while feeling only mildly attracted at first. Over time, their attraction to the other person *increased*. One smart, godly, and mature woman caught the eye of a friend of mine. Although he was only somewhat physically attracted to her, they became boyfriend and girlfriend. After they married and adopted two children from Southeast Asia, his desire for her skyrocketed as he saw how well she mothered their children. As his esteem grew for her, so did her allure. She became *one hot mama* in his eyes.

It works the opposite way, too. Have you ever met a mega-hot guy or gal, learned unsavory details about that person's life, and lost respect and attraction for him or her? As Shakespeare wrote, "All that glisters is not gold."[3] Without mincing words, Cloud and Townsend note that mature dating decisions are based on your values, not on specific physical attributes.[4]

Don't be fooled by movies and magazines. They push us to seek only tens on the attraction-o-meter, but desire is not all or none. Instead, picture it as a range zero to ten. Zero means there is not an ounce of sex appeal while a ten means you are twitterpated every time your eyes connect. The salient question is, what number on the scale of physical appeal is necessary for you to go out with them? It would be blasé to dine with a one or two, but could you eat sushi rolls and edamame with a date who is a five or six?

Keep sexual chemistry on your list but not near the top, and don't cross off your list too quickly that person you aren't initially attracted to.

The Top Value to Pursue

I used to scoff at Christians who fell prey to the temptation of romancing outside of their religion. Then I courted a non-Christian woman for a short time. (The enemy loves it when we judge others!) She was stunning, exotic, and spoke with a tantalizing accent. I still find it incredulous how my conviction to follow God's mandate quickly turned into muddy waters after meeting her. I only needed to refer back to my nonnegotiable list where the first item I listed was "Strong faith in Christ." My values were clear, but feelings are sneaky. The Bible states, "The heart is more deceitful than all else and is desperately sick; who can understand it?" (Jer. 17:9). My heart was deceived, but I'm thankful I had enough spiritual wherewithal to break it off.

God's primary concern is that we marry someone who shares our faith in Jesus: "Do not be unequally yoked with unbelievers. For what partnership has righteousness with lawlessness? Or what fellowship has light with darkness?" (2 Cor. 6:14 ESV). One translation says, "How can light live with darkness?" (NLT). Shared core values, interests, and sexual attraction are important when searching for a mate. At the same time, Gary Thomas reminds us that our "first priority, according to Scripture, is to find a spiritually compatible person."[5] I know several individuals who dismissed

God's command and sought singles outside their faith. They justi-
fied their decision with, "Christian guys weren't asking me out," or
"God will use our relationship so my fiancé will come to faith in
Christ." Hogwash.

One woman was ministering in Indonesia when she met an
attractive local man. She fell in love, married him, then converted
to *his* religion. The last time I checked, that was the *opposite* of
missionary work. God wants us to seek and save the lost, not marry
them. This is one of the reasons why having that nonnegotiable list
made out helps us keep our values intact.

My friends and I once laughed that we could "flirt to convert"
if we encountered a spellbinding woman who didn't follow the
Lord. But that joke ends quickly. And research backs that up. In one
study, for example, the chance of divorce skyrockets (61 percent)
when evangelicals marry someone with no religion.[6] Similarly,
mainline Protestants who marry someone without any religious
affiliation have a 63 percent chance of divorce.[7]

A vibrant marriage takes a truckload of work between two
healthy Christians, let alone when they begin a marriage on two
different foundations. The good news is that, according to Bradford
Wilcox, director of the National Marriage Project, "'active conservative protestants' who attend church regularly are actually 35%
less likely to divorce than those who have no religious preferences."[8]
The key is being "active" in your faith. What is also surprising is
that the chances of divorce go way up if people claim they follow
Christ but don't attend church regularly.[9] In other words, dedica-
tion to Christ and community help you stay married, but dabbling
in your faith and church increases your risk of divorce.[10]

Virtues Are Invaluable

Make sure your list contains someone who values not only a *confession* of Christ but a *commitment* to being like Him. It takes work to develop the character of Christ. Paul wrote to Timothy: "train yourself for godliness" (1 Tim. 4:7 ESV). That attractive man or woman might pump iron or loyally attend Zumba classes five times a week, but does he or she study the Bible, pray, and meet with other believers to "live their lives as Jesus did" (1 John 2:6 NLT)?

You find the specific traits to look for in Galatians 5:22–23: "The fruit of the Spirit is love, joy, peace, patience, kindness, goodness, faithfulness, gentleness, self-control; against such things there is no law." Again, a person's "hotness" and gregarious personality might pull you in like a tractor beam from *Star Trek*, but you won't stay long in the relationship if inner beauty doesn't match outer appeal.

Other virtues like purity and holiness might sound old school, but they never go out of style. With rampant sexual immorality in our culture, make sure your list contains a date who has learned self-control and embraces holiness. It doesn't mean this man or woman (or you) has never struggled with lust, masturbation, or sexual promiscuity, but make sure the biggest vices are in the past. You can make anything an addiction, even Netflix, social media, and fitness. Each addiction differs in its consequences, but for the most egregious kinds, let the person experience freedom for a minimum of six months before you consider dating.

A kindhearted Christian man who was recovering from a gambling addiction courted my friend's sister. For years he fought to break free but fell short until he found a supportive church community, accountability, and discipleship. He pursued this young woman while he was recovering, but she was rightfully wary. After several months of freedom, she allowed him to date her. Today they are happily married, and he hasn't made any bets since. Notice that she didn't play games with her heart (or his) and date him while hoping he would overcome his addiction. She waited, observed his life, received counsel, and then went out with him when he was healthy.

Character is key. You have your own relationship with Christ to cultivate without needing to worry about theirs. Therefore make sure your list contains dating someone you don't have to disciple. They won't be your pet project so you can address any unhealthy caretaker need inside of you. Mentoring your boyfriend or girl-friend won't be satisfying for long, because sooner or later you'll want an equal.

Instead, marry someone whose character and faith you admire. You don't get to choose someone else's future, even if what you want for them is good. Always date who someone *is*, not who you *want* them to be.

Got Grit?

Perseverance is often overlooked in favor of sex appeal, but it shouldn't be. Perseverance, or its twin, fortitude, is about staying power. To me, someone who has developed staying power is im-mensely sexier than a flaky, model-like wife or husband. A person might be eye candy, but will he or she be there until "death do us part?" In Wild West terms, perseverance is the grit that pushes you to dig in your boot heels when life gets tough. It's the ability to *overcome*. People who embody determination don't quit when faced with adversity in relationships. They aren't casual in their commitments. You can trust people with grit because they won't fold under pressure. Practically speaking, divorce isn't in their vocabulary. They are "in it to win it," no matter what.

My grandparents understood the power of perseverance. Throughout seventy-one years of marriage, they endured financial hardships, the death of loved ones, and uncertain economic times. Through each trial, they remained committed to each other. But I am often tempted by what is bigger, better, brighter, and faster. Maybe you can relate. We get mesmerized by the latest electronic gadget, are enticed to buy shiny new cars, or make it mandatory to don the latest fashion trend. Buying new clothes is mostly insignificant, but this kind of transitory thinking is dangerous when it spills into frequently changing churches, careers or—dare I say—boyfriends and girlfriends?

Galatians 6:9 reminds us "not [to] become discouraged in doing good, for in due time we will reap, if we do not become weary." And James 5:11 states that "we count those blessed who endured." Look for signs that your potential mate has the power to stay when things get tough. You'll gain respect for a person if you learn he or she endured the death of a loved one, completed a degree, overcame a personal obstacle, learned to play an instrument, or found freedom from addiction before even meeting you. These are significant indicators of fortitude.

French Fries and Friendship

There are more to lists than character, faith, and attraction. Your list must contain "fun" and "friendship." Just because you take an afternoon stroll with a guy who can quote Paul's entire letter to the Colossians doesn't mean you like being with him. Besides someone's noble qualities, it's just as important to find yourself laughing with your date.

Similarly, it's all too easy to get caught up in physical attraction or the avalanche of emotions and forget about friendship. As a wise woman said about marriage, "There's only so much sex you can have before you need to talk to each other." What my mom meant was that you and your partner need to be friends. At first, I reacted with an *Ewwww!* But what she said is true. I have met only a few daters in the West who don't want to be best friends with their spouse someday. Although friendship means different things to different people, most people want to be able to stick a french fry up their nose and get a good laugh—or maybe that's just me?

I see many marriages suffer because the husband and wife stopped being friends. Research agrees: at least two major studies reveal that a primary reason couples divorce is because they grow apart.[11] Thwart the possibility of divorce by listing *friendship* as a nonnegotiable. Sharing fun activities throughout your dating relationship and into your marriage will keep you connected. Every couple needs two to three common interests to enjoy together, such as hiking, biking, thrifting, running, sailing, or watching movies. One wife and husband might love cooking gourmet meals together, while another relishes RV trips. You pick—it's your relationship. What are two fun activities you hope to share with your boyfriend or girlfriend?

If you have next to nothing in common with an otherwise mature person, dig up a new activity and learn it together. Sign up for a lesson on volcano boarding, shaving alpacas, or topiary (the art of shaping shrubs and trees into animals).

Must Kayak?

You might want a man or woman with the same specific calling as yours. If you are seeking a date who works in your same field or ministry, be careful not to limit yourself. Your values may change over time, and so will your list. Vocations vary throughout life and specific passions may be stamped with expiration dates.

One of my female acquaintances desires to marry a man who is equally called to sports ministry. Athletics is a powerful way to share the gospel, and many people come to God through sports. However, I would challenge her to consider whether there is a less specific value that honors her heart but also doesn't paint a man with too narrow a brushstroke. Why not find a guy who likes to stay fit? It's reasonable that a man who has a passion for exercise would also be open to joining her for basketball, soccer, volleyball, or whatever sport she specializes in.

I'd never try to pry a God-honoring calling from someone's hand. If she truly planned on committing to a specific sports ministry and desires someone who wants the same thing, then she should hold to her conviction. Perhaps she could even consider whether staying unmarried is the better relationship route to take. But if the type of ministry is for only a season in life, then it's best to broaden your value and keep as many doors open as possible.

After absorbing a sermon several years ago, I was inspired to jump on a plane with a new life mission. The guest speaker delivered a passionate message about millions of people in an Asian country who don't own Bibles and showed how we could help. As my girlfriend and I drove from the church afterward, I was still on fire for the project. *Where do I sign up? Should I quit my job?*

She listened but didn't share my level of excitement.

What? How could sharing the Word of God not be your top priority right now?

Her lackadaisical attitude toward my new mission irked me and caused a fight. At that moment, I thought, *How can I marry someone who doesn't share the same zeal about providing Bibles to the lost in far East Asia?* A few weeks later my feelings died down. Though I am still passionate about overseas missions, I don't need to date a woman who mirrors my exact calling; I need someone who loves people from other cultures.

Comb through your list. Did you write any laser-like items that might stunt your dating endeavors? Pray. Ask God which of them need to be widened and which you need to hold onto. Remember, many of our values change in intensity and duration over time. Life happens. Passions change. People get sick and can't travel. Girlfriends and boyfriends get married. Friends move to other cities. Kids change everything.

Make sure you have distilled your values down to the broadest form and match someone with those. Gary Thomas notes, "You won't know what the future holds, but you *can* know the kind of character you're marrying."[12] Deeper and broader values will endure the test of time, but it's up to you to decide how you complete your list.

That's why I was shocked to discover one man who broke up with a woman because she didn't like kayaking. *Really? How much of your life revolves around kayaking?* But he considered it a nonnegotiable trait. I wonder what a more significant value could be for him? Maybe someone who is active or likes the outdoors? Couldn't they have found one of the other million activities couples enjoy together? Perhaps he was called to a kayaking ministry in Pokhara, Nepal.

Your list should keep as many relationship doors open as possible while considering who God wired you to be. It's not my place to thwart the unique values on your list—only to make sure it was *God* who inspired them.

Bible Barbie and Frankenstein

My mentor was right in saying that it's imperative to be continually moving *toward* some values while moving *away* from others. The goal is to align your values to God's values. Again, just because you value something doesn't make it valuable—it only means *you* find it important. Some of the traits on your list have merit but don't hold the greatest importance. Others are merely fantastical. Forgive me for using the following stereotypes.

I can testify that many men look for a combination of traits in a woman based on unrealistic expectations. Guys often seek a wife who displays bold faith and selfless love like Mother Teresa, prepares meals like Rachael Ray, and displays the exquisite beauty of Miss America. I've heard this flawless creature called *Bible Barbie.* But she doesn't exist. These women you date won't look like Barbie, just as you don't look like Ken. Besides, a real-life Barbie is anatomically impossible, and her actual body fat percentage would be associated with anorexia.[13]

Closer to God's heart is finding someone who has a genuine heart to serve, not a date who slavishly dotes on you 24/7 (see Gen. 2:18). More important than a woman who can prepare five-star meals seven days a week is pursuing a woman who genuinely desires to care for her home (see 1 Tim. 5:14). Men can be equal partners in this, of course. You'll find more joy in seeking a woman who lives a healthy lifestyle and exhibits inner beauty rather than one who reflects the impossible measurements in your head (see 1 Peter 3:3–4).

If you're a woman, you're not off the hook, either. You might imagine a man with the income of Elon Musk, the muscles of Dwayne "The Rock" Johnson, and the influential title of "senior pastor." You can't amalgamate the best features from previous boyfriends into a fictional boyfriend—yours will be Frankenstein. Please don't marry Frankenstein. He ravaged German villages and people were scared of him.

Although a man's high salary might reveal a solid work ethic, the Lord doesn't value a seven-figure income nearly as much as a man who is faithful at whatever job he does to provide for his family (see 1 Tim. 5:8). More valuable than a man with the placard of CEO on his desk is a man who gives 100 percent at his place of work—even if he wears a nametag on his uniform (see Prov. 12:11). Chiseled abs might catch your eye but pale in comparison to a man who avoids sexual sin and considers his body a "temple of the Holy Spirit" (1 Cor. 6:19).

Seek traits for your list not only that Scripture supports but also will stand the test of time. Place less important attributes like titles, income, and body type on your negotiables list.

Is it possible to find a match in whom you've checked off every box on your list? My female friend who went overboard with her hundred-item wish list astonishingly married a man who fulfilled every single requirement. But she didn't end up with a storybook marriage. We are all fallen people who will marry someone just as flawed, needy, and unfinished as we are. No one on this side of heaven was designed to meet *all* of our desires—far from it. Perfect people don't exist. And spouses make horrible saviors anyway.

Let God Color in Your Spouse

Lists answer the question, *What do I find important in life and what kind of mate do I want?* Take time fine-tuning yours and let these answers be a guide. Write your list but don't worship it. Be judicious with your immutable values, writing most items in pencil, not pen. Allow your list to be an outline and let God color in the details of the person. Your future spouse will be far more colorful and dynamic than a list will ever encompass, so give God permission to add, subtract, and modify it frequently. Review it with Him often so you won't miss a potential mate.

Make sure you apply the list to yourself. It's appropriate to expect virtues like commitment, financial stability, perseverance, and integrity, but do *you* embody them? Lists won't work if they don't first gauge your own life. Where do you need to grow? Andy Stanley rightly observes, "Is it just me, or is there something a bit hypocritical about wanting something in someone else that you've not been willing to develop in yourself?"[14]

Don't forget to write down *having fun* with the person you date. If you rush to discover if a man or woman checks off every item on your list too soon, a hilarious date playing mini-golf will mutate into an interview at best and interrogation at worst. And stay a mile away from this Homer Simpson moment: someone I know once wrote all their nonnegotiables on yellow sticky notes, handed the stack to the woman he was dating, and nonchalantly asked her if she checked all the boxes. That's never a good idea. She wasn't thrilled and cut off communication with him.

Remember that you probably won't know what someone truly values until you date them. Healthy relationships are just as much (if not more) about the kind of relationship you form *together* as they are about the specific person you choose. Seek someone who loves Jesus, exudes solid character, and can stick a french fry up their nose. Finally, be prepared to address the list that your special guy or gal will bring into the relationship as well.

A Dangerous Prayer

As we saw in Chapter 1, Christian marriage is founded on a covenant mindset, not a consumer one. One way to combat a worldly list is to ask God to provide a spouse:

> Who, with you, will glorify God more than if you were both
>   single;
> Whom you can serve;
> Who will encourage you to become more like Christ;
> Who will bring you joy (as opposed to happiness);
> Who, with you, will advance God's kingdom.

Try that dating prayer on for size. See if these criteria don't sing harmony with your spirit, glorify God, and slap a selfish marriage culture in the face.

CHAPTER 8

Unfriend-Zoning People and Other Ways to Meet Dates

Don't wait for the right opportunity: create it.
—ATTRIBUTED TO GEORGE BERNARD SHAW

I read about a guy who drove to his date's house to pick her up for their first scheduled night out. But when he walked to the front door and knocked, a different woman greeted him. His date's sister confessed that she wasn't home because she was spending time with another guy. *Really?* Instead of walking away in a sulk, he said, "Do you want to go out then?" She agreed, and they eventually married.[1] If that's not the epitome of making the best from an awkward situation, I don't know what is.

Shrugging his shoulders, my mentor told me, "I don't know how you'll meet your spouse, Eric. You could meet her at the gas station."

There are innumerable ways you could meet your future husband or wife. The key is to be creative, try new ideas, and stay open to however God wants to work.

> A tiny spark of attraction has the potential to turn into a flame if you begin noticing their integrity, boldness, love for God, and servant heart toward others.

Random encounters aren't the only way God brings people together. Romance often requires work. If you desire to marry, don't wait on God to do something He asks *you* to do. Proverbs 18:22 says, "He who *finds* a wife finds a good thing and obtains favor from the LORD" (emphasis added). In Hebrew, the word *finds* is *masa*—a verb than means "to find, attain."[2] In this context, it clearly denotes to "meet" and "marry."[3] *Masa* equals action, but that doesn't mean you're taking your love life into your own hands. It's doing what you can, *with* God, to get married. As you date, "the LORD your God is with you wherever you go" (Josh. 1:9). The same Holy Spirit who brought Rachel to Jacob and Rebekah to Isaac is the One who arranges you and your future spouse to sit next to each other in class, begin exchanging messages online, or bump into each other at a gas station.

But don't leave your love life to chance. If you've allowed God to work on your character and feel that you're spiritually and emotionally ready to meet someone, then you have a green light to date.

Five Practical Ways to Meet People

You can meet people in countless ways, but here are five fresh takes on new and old methods.

Method 1: Unfriend-Zone Someone

Friends are friends for a reason. You share common interests, enjoy stimulating conversations, and do fun things together. Since friendship is the basis of marriage, it's reasonable to consider someone already inside your social circle who may be a good match but whom you prematurely imprisoned in the friend-zone. Maybe they were axed because they're not your preferred physical type. Or you believe your personalities would clash since you're quiet and they're outspoken. But differences needn't be solved before going on a first date. A tiny spark of attraction has the potential to turn into a flame if you begin noticing their integrity, boldness, love for God, and servant heart toward others. So if you have already built a friendship with a godly man or woman, consider unfriend-zoning them and going on one or two dates.

Write down five to ten godly and mature friends you've crossed off as potential mates. Review your list. Do some names still make you cringe? Do any make you wonder? Pray about each name. Did God speak to your heart on any particular person? Maybe a diamond got lumped in with the coal? Sometimes God will open your eyes to a man or woman you've known for years and give you a revamped spousal lens to see them through. If this is you, make a move to let them know you're interested. Go on one or two dates and see how you relate to them now as a potential romantic partner. Take it from there. If the dates are a dud, thank them for their time. You can put them back in friend-jail and throw away the key.

Method 2: Network and Ask for Help

With so many available men and women waiting to get married, there's no shortage of potential wives or husbands at your gym, job, or church. The problem is, how do you know if they are single, looking to date, or even share the same faith? Just because you attend a big church bursting at the seams with singles doesn't mean you know each other. In Sunday services, the available thirty-somethings sitting in the back-left corner might as well be as far away as South Korea from those who congregate in the balcony. Even if an attractive guy or gal catches your eye only a few rows over, you may still encounter invisible social boundaries that keep you from crossing the 38th parallel.

Plan A is to walk up, say "hi," and introduce yourself—this is always a bold and respectable approach, as I did with the young lady at my dentist's office. If you need more information, do some Sherlocking on your potential date. Find a pastor, leader, or friend who knows them and get some good intel. If what you discover is intriguing, return to plan A, or initiate plan B. Plan B is asking a friend or leader who knows both of you to set you up on a date. This method is not a cop-out. Leveraging your network to help you date shows both wisdom and humility. As one wise proverb states, "When pride comes, then comes dishonor; but with the humble there is wisdom" (Prov. 11:2). Plan B is also beneficial because the facilitator can vouch for each of your characters. You'll have a much better chance of landing a date with their stamp of approval.

If no one in your network is catching your eye, approach a friend or a married couple you respect to see if they know of anyone who might be a good match. If you give it a moment's thought, you probably know someone who enjoys playing matchmaker. Ask God to bring to mind someone who can help. Then follow up with something like, "Hey, Nick and Karen. Do you know anyone who could be a good match for me? Here's what I'm looking for in a spouse." Then give them your list of nonnegotiables. After they read it, see if they know anyone who fits the bill. If so, have them help you connect. If not, or if you've already crossed off the people they mention, at least they have your list for posterity.

Another option is to ask a leader in the church to become pro-active in helping the singles near you find each other. Start sponsoring gatherings for unmarried men and women in the church to get to know each other. Coordinate an evening of speed dating sessions for the church's unmarrieds. Or if you attend a smaller church, maybe see if a number of churches in the area would coordinate their efforts.

If they aren't interested, where else do they expect Christian men and women to find their spouses—bars? clubs? I get the church leadership's dilemma: if they pair up the singles and the relationship crashes and burns, they fear the fallout. But mature single Christians won't blame a leader or a friend for setting them up. In fact, they'll thank them for trying.

We can't avoid the frequent messiness of dating, but the church is still the best place for Christians to meet and develop a relationship.

Method 3: Join a New Group

If you're tired of not finding a quality date in your congregation or local area, consider befriending another group elsewhere. One guy I heard of started driving an hour each way to attend a Bible study with people he barely knew. He not only wanted some fresh, positive friendships but also to get married. Through those new connections, he met a wonderful lady and they began dating. Today, they are married and have a beautiful family. Sometimes, you must take drastic steps to find a date. It might be painful or scary to break the safe boundaries of your local community and enlarge your social circle. Meeting new people in other zip codes isn't convenient, but finding love is worth the inconvenience.

Another more convenient option is to join a new group closer to home. Unless you live in a small town, there will be plenty of available men and women you don't know who aren't too far away. Find a friend who is part of a mixed-gender group and start spending time with them. You can always search online for meet-up groups, shared-interest groups on social media, and recurring social events in your area. Some groups hike, work out, cook, or learn how to paint watercolors together. Pick a group, take a friend with you, and commit to going for three months. Keep your eyes and heart open to see if anyone there could be your potential spouse.

Method 4: Start Your Own Themed Group

If you can't find a group you like, start a themed group yourself. Pick something you enjoy—a book you want to read, an activity you're fond of (ultimate frisbee, anyone?), or a weekly meet-up for foodies at the new bistro in town. Be sure to gather at least three or four times a month to give ample time for people to get to know each other. Remember, this group has the dual purpose of engaging in an activity you like to do *and* finding a date. To advertise, make the group official with your church, list it on social media, and spread it through word of mouth.

The silver lining is that even if you don't land a date, you'll enjoy the subject matter. And you'll probably gain a new friend or two in the process. These friends likely know other singles, too.

Another plus is that if romance does ignite with someone in the group, you'll share at least one interest. Bible studies are the quintessential group for Christians, and for a good reason—what's better to have in common than a love for Jesus and Scripture?

Method 5: Electronic Affections

There's no shortage of single men and women on the internet. Online dating doesn't just expand your social circle, it explodes it. Unless you set geographical limits on your dating profile, you can meet singles from your city, state, and from Zimbabwe to New Zealand. If the program allows, you can filter people based upon any number of criteria, including age, religion, whether they already have kids or want kids, and if they're willing to relocate.

The unwritten rule in online dating is that it's nonexclusive in nature, so you can get to know several different men or women in a short time. It wouldn't be uncommon in online dating if you went on three first dates with different people in the same week (just don't repeat my friend's blunder and go on three separate dates on the same day).

If you dwell in a tight-knit community where gossip never sleeps, connecting with potential marriage partners online can add a layer of privacy to your love life. If you're meeting singles outside your area, Aunt Polly won't even know you went on a date, started a relationship, or broke up. Likewise, your local Bible study will experience less collateral damage if two members start dating and the relationship doesn't work out. In fact, in online dating, if things don't go past the first date, you may never see them again. Of course, if you start a relationship, you won't want to stay incognito forever and will have to introduce them to your community at some point.

An integral part of online dating is to meet fast and date slow. The sooner you schedule a date, the better. You want to interact with them in person fast, because most important is experiential knowledge, not the smattering of facts you read on their profile page. From texting, their wit might shine through, but you need to see their mannerisms firsthand, hear the tone of their voice, and observe how they treat others.

One of the main risks of messaging for months without a proper date is that your heart can become attached too early to the *idea* of that person, not to who they really are. Even talking on the phone and video-calling isn't enough and can give you a false sense of knowing someone. Personal experience aligns your thoughts with reality. According to Dallas Willard, "Knowledge is the capacity to represent things as they are, on an appropriate basis of thought and experience."[4]

When you do schedule a date for the first time, they may be vastly different from who you thought they were. For example, they may seem to be kindhearted from short phone conversations, but how do they treat the server at your restaurant? You'd never know they were immature until you see them berate the waiter for filling their glass with Pepsi instead of Dr. Pepper. Meeting a person you connect with online can be shocking, but it's better for your heart to be surprised only after a week or two, not six months. Therefore, meet sooner rather than later.

On the other hand, surprises can be positive too. Your date could be more dashing and debonair in person than their profile ever showed, so it's okay to be excited to meet them.

If you continue going on dates, take it slowly. Observe their life for a while. Since you don't share mutual friends, church, or often even the same city, developing a shared context adds time to the getting-to-know-you process. Two people from different backgrounds can be like two worlds colliding—like when the two circles begin to overlap in the Venn diagram. In online dating, go on several nonexclusive dates before committing to the exclusive-dating stage.

What to Know Before You Sign Up

Online dating apps vary in scope and purpose. Make sure you find one where people are looking to get married, not just wanting to "meet new people." The paid programs have a bigger pool of singles and filters for matches, and they are filled with more people who are intentionally looking for marriage. The adage is true—*You get what you pay for.* The website doesn't need to be overtly Christian, but make sure you search for someone who shares your faith.

As you create a profile, consider the following questions:

Does what I wrote sound like me?
What length of time am I committing to this website or app?
How much time do I have to give to this each week?
How far am I willing to travel to meet someone?
If I fall in love, am I willing to move to their city, state,
    or country?

Per the first question, complete your profile with honesty and humility, and put your best self forward. It's not a CV or a personal journal, so avoid listing every certification or writing a ten-page autobiography. More don'ts include writing about personal struggles, tragic events, or romantic failures. It's not that you can't be authentic, but it's about being wise in what you share upfront. The purpose of your profile isn't about you, anyway—it's about the man or woman you're trying to meet.

Your goal is to showcase the best information about yourself so a potential mate can decide whether you're the kind of person they'd want to date. They can learn about your skeletons in the closet later. However your life has been, show yourself as a happy person who is friendly, committed to Christ, and able to take care of yourself. The person reading about you wants to know you are ready and capable of love. Therefore, don't be shy about listing your positive personality traits, your passions, and the places you volunteer. If you don't believe how amazing and incredible you are, remind yourself what God thinks about you: "I praise you, for I am fearfully and wonderfully made" (Ps. 139:14 ESV). Recruit your friends to help you develop your profile. Ask them for what they believe are your top five positive traits.

You'll also need at least one quality picture of yourself. Choose photos that represent you naturally, not the one where you're posing with your back to the camera, pensively looking to the left, holding the corner of your Ray-Ban sunglasses. Likewise, limit selfies because they come across as vain. Choose pictures farther than arm's length and ones in which you're smiling. Profile pictures can be as simple as showing you in your favorite part of town or at work, doing your favorite hobby, playing music, or being with your family. And post one from your inner-city mission trip or your travels abroad. Generally speaking, potential online matches want to see that you're leading a fulfilling life and one they would like to join. If you are in a lull right now and can't list anything interesting, then as my friend Marvin recommended, "Start doing something that is cool." Begin a hobby, and, after a few weeks, update your profile.

Take your time and be intentional about filling out your information completely. Sparse profiles will beam a lax attitude to your potential dates; worse, it'll portray you as lazy. Have a friend review it and give you feedback. Finally, look at your profile and ask yourself this crucial question: "Would *I* want to go out with me?"

Next, consider how much time you'll commit to this website. I would devote at least three to six months to electronic setups and go on dates with as many different people as your schedule allows. Meet a variety of people and choose to ask out singles who don't look like a perfect match but share the same faith. If you aren't receiving a truckload of matches and the dates are scarce, stay committed to the process anyway. Think of this: you only need to meet *one* right person. So give online dating enough time and space for that potentially perfect person to pop up.

Think about how much time you can set aside to get to know people, because you don't want it to feel like a full-time job. If you can invest five hours a week, get to know only a few people at a time. The goal isn't to talk to a lot of people, it's to *meet* them. Years ago, I contacted so many single women on a dating site that I had to create a spreadsheet to keep everyone straight. How many conversations are too many at once? Answer: when you need a spreadsheet. Overall, keep your number of current contacts to a number you can handle, and once you go out on a date, highlight their name or delete them from your list.

How far you're willing to travel is also a huge factor in online dating. An Australian woman or a French man might allure you with their accent, but are you ready to go to Sydney or Paris to meet them? Is that wise? Consider your motives—potential dates are looking to get married just like you, and they don't need another pen pal. Pray about how far you're willing to travel, get counsel, and be clear with your boundaries on your profile. If you might be open to meeting someone abroad, get to know them and find out. After a few weeks, if you become disinterested or know you'd never visit where they live, inform them sooner rather than later. Also, there's nothing wrong if you want to stay where you live and aren't willing to uproot your life. Dating is easier, safer, and certainly cheaper if you can meet someone within your area anyway.

Finally, treat everyone you're talking to online with the same respect you would give them if you were talking to them in person. They are people, not products or a means to an end. It's easy to forget that every profile is an actual person created in God's image (see Gen. 1:27). They have hopes, dreams, and fears, just as you do. Communicate in a way that honors them. As the Bible says, "Don't look out only for your own interests, but take an interest in others, too" (Phil. 2:4 NLT).

If you don't want to continue meeting someone after a few chats, thank them for their time and let them know you're not interested in pursuing anything further. Otherwise, they'll wonder, *What happened? Where did that person go?* and *Did I do something wrong?* Every context is different, so you don't need to send a break-up email if you've only exchanged courtesies. If you ever wonder how you should communicate with your matches, follow the Golden Rule: "In everything, therefore, treat people the same way you want them to treat you, for this is the Law and the Prophets" (Matt. 7:12).

Finally, be cautious with online dating. Not everyone is who they say they are on their profile. Some online singles have ulterior motives, such as wanting sex, money, or another romantic feather in their cap. If you're wary about meeting a complete stranger, make sure you do it in a public space or bring a friend for backup.

How to Have a Good First Date

Whether you connected online or through friends, plan the first date well. If you're a guy and you're not sure what she would like, have a couple of options ready and present them to her. Most women cringe if you show up and say, "I didn't plan anything. What do you want to do?"

Overall, keep your initial get-together simple and casual. Save the knockout dress and suave suit for formal galas after you've committed to each other. Otherwise, you'll feel anxious and stuffy when you meet. Plus, if you make reservations at the nicest restaurant in town on the outset, what's left for the encore? The goal on the first date isn't to impress, but to interact. Hence keep the first date relaxed and plan something easy where you can get to know each other. They will know you are a quality person by your thoughtful plan, your questions, and your listening skills, not by your overspending.

Afternoon dates are light and easy. Meeting in the daytime is not just safer but also easier on the pocketbook. Examples include the classic coffee date, a short hike, a walk in the park, eating tapas outside, or indulging in dark chocolate cherry frozen yogurt. Add zest to a coffee date by picking out a new game together at a toy store, then competing over lattes. The hidden benefit to afternoon dates is that if you're having a blast after a couple of hours and suddenly it's close to dinnertime, you can ask if they'd like to extend the date to dinner.

Traditional evening dates on a Friday or Saturday night tend to be more romantic and classier. They also display a stronger level of interest than sharing a smoothie at 2:00 p.m. Whether you plan on an afternoon or evening date, pairing food with a fun activity before or after dinner adds variety to the event. Snooping around a museum, viewing animals at the zoo, or attending an art fair also gives you a chance to get to know the person in a different context. If you've been a good listener, chances are you already know at least one thing they like to do. Another bonus is that an activity takes the pressure off when you're intermittently focused on something outside of yourself—like when you're taking pictures with the wallaby in front of the marsupial habitat.

Another first date rule is to avoid *marathon dates*. These are sunup to sundown dates that are way too long. You never want to wear out your welcome, so keep the initial meeting on the shorter side. At the far end, four hours is plenty of time for food and an activity. But even sixty minutes of focused conversation is sufficient for singles to know whether they want to see each other again. If you like each other, keeping it on the shorter side will leave room for the anticipation to build until your next date. But rules like this are made to be broken—if you're both having an absolute blast, there's no reason not to extend a date—just make sure they have time to do so.

Ending a first date can be awkward, so plan beforehand what you will or won't say. If the date is coming to a close and you don't want to go out again, don't lead them on. Only make promises you can keep. Say, "I'll call you," or "I'd like to go out again," or "I'll message you," if you mean it. But neither of you should automatically expect a second date. You know you became too emotionally invested too soon if you're crushed by their lack of interest in going out again. Either you were in a friendlationship beforehand or romantic fantasies got the best of you. Here's a respectful line my mentor taught me years ago to end a date when you don't plan on going out again: "Thanks for giving me a chance to get to know you."

The other scenario is if you're considering a second date but need to think and pray about where your heart is. Tell them the truth. Use something like, "I had fun, but can I have a few days to consider what I want next?" If this is you, be sure to initiate another meet-up or let them know, "I'm not interested in going further" or "I'd like to go out again."

Know You

As I've said before, there's no one right way to date, just many wrong ones. Unfriend-zoning someone, getting help from family or friends, joining a group, starting a group, and online dating are all right ways. God allows them all. The key is to know what works for you. Challenge yourself. If you've prayed, and God has given you the okay to date, put yourself out there and try a new way to meet your spouse. You won't know the result unless you try.

Don't lose track of your goal. It doesn't matter how you meet; the aim is to have an amazing marriage, not a courtship that reflects a Hollywood romance.

CHAPTER 9

Sex, True Purity, and Almost Jumping Out of a Moving Car

Love is patient.
—1 Corinthians 13:4

I was eighteen and stuck in my mom's car when, out of the blue, she hit me with, "Eric, I have something to share with you. When you date, remember two things: keep it in your pants and don't impregnate anyone."

I gasped for air, completely stunned and unable to unhear the unthinkable. My head spun to the window, and I calculated how many times my body would roll on the pavement if I jumped out. The mature part of me knew she was right—I needed to avoid sex and not make any life-altering mistakes. But still . . . all I could react with was, "Mooooom!"

Her hallmark advice was over before I could protest. At least her one-way conversation was laconic and practical. But her "just don't do it" insight didn't give me much other helpful information.

My next experience with trying to figure out how best to manage my sex drive and treat women came in college. As a new believer and sex-hungry college student, I went to my priest for advice. After confessing my sins, we began discussing life on campus and the struggles of young Catholics.

"That's just what college kids do," he said.

Though I felt accepted, his response deflated me. But I also knew what he was trying say: *I hear your heart, Eric, but it's inevitable that young people will fool around.* In one sense, I appreciated his merciful approach to normalizing sexual desire in singles. At the same time, I was looking for solid biblical teaching and godly practical advice, not sentiment. At the other extreme, when I jumped into conservative evangelicalism a few years later, I quickly learned that the two cardinal sins were drinking alcohol and engaging in premarital sex. There was little grace to make mistakes. I grew leaps and bounds spiritually in my new church home, but I couldn't help feeling as though my security in Christ rested on nothing more than avoiding these sins.

To grow as a Christian, I was looking for more than the sentiment of the Catholic Church or the judgment I sometimes saw in evangelicalism. Unmarried men and women weren't being discipled in their sexuality.

Christian singles today are more confused about sex than ever. On one hand, our culture is swimming in sex. It's all around us on the internet, magazine ads, and television shows. Worse, pornography lures behind only a few clicks on the keyboard. But we are drowning in misinformation. Many in a godless culture downplay sex to an essential bodily need like eating food or breathing air.

We need holistic teaching on how to develop a healthy

Christian sexual ethic based on Scripture—minus the Bible-thumping. Singles need wisdom, the best of neuroscience, and good ol' common sense as they navigate physical touch in this daunting dating culture.

What I found is that as you put your sexuality under God's sovereignty, you'll not only feel closer to Him but make better decisions and set yourself up for a healthy marriage.

Purity Is More than Keeping It in Your Pants

Developing a healthy Christian sexual ethic begins under the auspices of purity. I'm not talking about the kind of ring-wearing, chastity-belt-hugging, self-flagellating, superficial outer purity that seeks only to keep you out of the gossip circle. Purity doesn't begin with sex at all; it's a wholeheartedness toward God. Purity is a laser-like devotion to Christ and His ways. It has the singular focus of pleasing Him and living under an audience of One. Purity includes avoiding ignominious activities—but more than that, it is a heart to know God in an uncorrupted fashion.

Like the apostle Paul, we need to say, "Whatever were gains to me I now consider loss for the sake of Christ" (Phil. 3:7 NIV). He wanted to know one thing—Jesus. That's why the Lord said, "Blessed are the pure in heart, for they will see God" (Matt. 5:8). As seminary professor Craig Blomberg states, "The 'pure in heart' exhibit a single-minded devotion to God that stems from the internal cleansing created by following Jesus."[1]

Devotion to Christ means that we allow God to transform us from the inside out. Sexual purity is a natural flow of the inner kind, "for from the overflow of the heart the mouth speaks" (Matt 12:34 TLV). But focusing only on the external is taking the dead-end road of the Pharisees. They were so obsessed with doing the right things that they failed to be the right *kind* of person. Legalism, therefore, is born from a neglected heart and an idolized outward appearance. Jesus rightly chastised these indignant finger pointers: "You clean the outside of the cup and dish, but inside they are full of greed and self-indulgence" (Matt. 23:25 NIV). What is most alarming is not your battle with sex but that you can do all the right things and still be far from God.

The good news is that "now in Christ Jesus, you who were far away have been brought near by the blood of Christ" (Eph. 2:13 CSB). Purity is impossible to achieve on your own merits, because it is the blood of Christ, not your own actions, that reconciles you to God. Whether you've avoided hitting a home run before marriage or slept with the entire team, your state of spiritual depravity is simply too wrecked for abstinence to fix. Titus 3:5 states, "[Jesus] saved us, not because of righteous things we had done, but because of his mercy. He saved us through the washing of rebirth and renewal by the Holy Spirit" (NIV). He came to cleanse the inside of your cup.

Purity is allowing Him to wash your insides so they will sparkle. An inner radiance will undoubtedly shine through to your actions. In your reliance on Christ, you'll have the power to be "imitators of God" and to "walk in love" (Eph. 5:1–2). Because your and God's hearts are aligned, you won't act on your temptations to have sex outside of God's will for it.

Inner and outer purity will require the best of our relationship with God. We must work hard to "walk with decency" and avoid "sexual impurity and promiscuity" (Rom. 13:13 CSB). We start this process by accepting what God has done for us and galvanizing our devotion to Him.

What If You've Gone Too Far?

If you've been promiscuous, God is offering you a giant reset button for your sexuality right now. Start by naming your sin, accepting God's forgiveness, and committing your body to Christ, for "if we confess our sins, He is faithful and righteous, so that He will forgive us our sins and cleanse us from all unrighteousness" (1 John 1:9).

Though sexual sin can cause considerable pain, this is the exact kind of sin for which Jesus died: "Though your sins are as scarlet, they shall become as white as snow; though they are red like crimson, they shall be like wool" (Isa. 1:18). Also, "He is so rich in kindness and grace that he purchased our freedom with the blood of his Son and forgave our sins" (Eph. 1:7 NLT). Repent, learn from your mistakes, and move on. Thankfully, God doesn't keep score, so neither should we. As Isaiah 43:25 states, "I—yes, I alone—will blot out your sins for my own sake and will never think of them again" (NLT).

Often, however, praying alone and asking for forgiveness without outside help isn't enough to feel absolution. God designed us to be open and honest with others so they can help us experience forgiveness. If you're plagued by guilt, taking action by confessing your sins to another will free you. My mentor said it like this: "Guilt means *do*." James says it this way: "Confess your sins to one another, and pray for one another so that you may be healed" (5:16).

Believe it or not, I miss the days when I would meet with the Roman Catholic priest to practice the sacrament of reconciliation. Afterward, I always felt better. I know we have only "one mediator between God and men" (1 Tim. 2:5 ESV). At the same time, it's scriptural that healing comes when we can bare our soul to someone who wants to listen to our struggle, pray for us, and won't judge our deepest and darkest secrets. I always walked away feeling much lighter and spiritually reset after meeting with the priest. Now I'm thankful I have close guy friendships where we can openly share our personal battles.

You might also need to make amends with the person with whom you went too far physically. Not only are forgiveness and reconciliation vertical, they are also horizontal. Whether it's typing an apology email or asking for forgiveness in person, the more experiential you can make forgiveness, the freer you'll feel. Don't get stuck wilting in the shadow of your sin; live in the light. Make it right with the people you sinned against where it's appropriate.

Depending on how much you were steeped in sexual sin, consider seeing a Christian counselor. It's freeing to share your sexual struggles with a caring professional. The therapist can also help you develop healthier patterns of behavior. You can't change the past, but you can still have a fulfilling sex life when you're married. Plus, you can use what you've learned through your mistakes to help others grow and avoid the same mistakes. What Satan meant for evil, God will use for good.

If you have not had sex, you are blessed indeed. In that area, you have pleased your Father in heaven by controlling [your] body (see 1 Thess. 4:4). He is proud of you. Consider your celibacy as a huge gift to God, yourself, and your future spouse. Your job now is to humbly teach others what you have learned and how you remained abstinent. With the grace you have received, pay it forward.

Regarding those who are virgins, a false teaching has snuck into the church called the sexual prosperity gospel. This heresy promises that if you remain sexually pure, then God will reward you with a spouse and a mind-blowing sex life. The truth is that you *might* marry the person of your dreams and experience an erotic sex life. But God's blessings are tied to His goodness, not your chastity. By waiting to have sex now, you aren't storing up God-bucks in heaven that you get to cash in on a wife or husband later. Our walk with Christ isn't a quid pro quo.

Likewise, God isn't in the business of being a business. If you've relegated your celibacy to some type of heavenly exchange—where you are trying to earn God's favor now for a scintillating sex life later—you're setting yourself up for failure. And you'll feel jaded with God. The Lord isn't interested in relating to you as Someone who provides you relationship goods and services bought with your obedience. Instead, He wants to be your Father. He's the kind of Father who says, "Before they call I will answer; while they are yet speaking I will hear" (Isa. 65:24 ESV). So stay sexually pure, resting in the complete love and acceptance of the Father, knowing that He sees how you've saved yourself.

Ultimately the greatest reward for a pure heart and a pure sexual life is knowing Him. How He explicitly chooses to bless your obedience is up to Him.

God, Sex, and the Bible

God loves sex. He created it. He loves it so much that the apostle Paul commanded husbands and wives to regularly practice it: "The husband should fulfill his wife's sexual needs, and the wife should fulfill her husband's needs" (1 Cor. 7:3 NLT). As one biblical commentator put it, "Physical lovemaking in marriage is as much part of what it means to 'honor God with your body' as refusing to go to bed with a prostitute (cf. 1 Cor. 6:15, 20)."[2] The Lord wanted Adam and Eve not only to have sex for procreation but for outrageous pleasure. Christian philosopher Peter Kreeft notes:

> The first two things we learn about sex from God, right from the beginning, are that God designed it, not man or society,

and that it is very good. The first command was, "Be fruit-
ful and multiply." I do not think God had in mind growing
oranges and memorizing times tables.[3]

Sex isn't dirty, and we shouldn't be ashamed of our bodies and
our sexual cravings. As Paul reminds us, "Everything created by
God is good, and nothing is to be rejected if it is received with gratitude; for it is sanctified by means of the word of God and prayer"
(1 Tim. 4:4–5). Consider Song of Solomon (also called Song of
Songs), a biblical erotic love poem between two newlyweds. It's
enough to make almost any reader blush. It was written to "express
the intimacy of the bond that exists between husband and wife."[4]
Check out this sampling:

How beautiful are your feet in sandals,
     O noble daughter!
Your rounded thighs are like jewels,
     the work of a master hand.
Your navel is a rounded bowl
     that never lacks mixed wine.
Your belly is a heap of wheat,
     encircled with lilies.
Your two breasts are like two fawns,
     twins of a gazelle. (7:1–3 ESV)

But sex is more than a physical union between spouses. If you
know Christ, He lives in you: "I have been crucified with Christ;
and it is no longer I who live, but Christ lives in me" (Gal. 2:20).
That is why the Bible is emphatic about what we do with our sexual
organs. Paul tells us:

Do you not know that your bodies are members of Christ himself? Shall I then take the members of Christ and unite them with a prostitute? Never! Do you not know that he who unites himself with a prostitute is one with her in body? For it is said, "The two will become one flesh." But whoever is united with the Lord is one with him in spirit." (1 Cor. 6:15–17 NIV)

The value God places on sexual integrity cannot be overstated in Scripture. Sexual immorality has a myriad of consequences, such as being "excluded from the life of God," putting you at risk for losing your "inheritance in the kingdom of Christ and God," and negatively affecting the wellbeing of other believers (Eph. 4:17–19; 5:5; 1 Cor. 5:6). Moreover, Romans 1 shows how idolatry often fuels sexual sin, which can lead to the "wrath of God" (vv. 18–27).

As followers of Jesus, we are to "flee sexual immorality," "flee from idolatry," and "flee from youthful lusts and pursue righteousness, faith, love, and peace with those who call on the Lord from a pure heart" (1 Cor. 6:18; 10:14; 2 Tim. 2:22). The Greek word for "flee" literally means to "move hastily from danger because of fear."[5] Don't we run away from anything that causes harm? Common sense tells us to. I'd take off like an Olympian if I met a swarm of killer bees, boiling lava, or a mama grizzly bear. Although our sinful nature and our culture do not portray it as an obvious danger, the Bible is

> Some argue that since neither Hebrew nor Greek have a specific word for "premarital sex" between two unmarried partners, it is not addressed in the Bible. That couldn't be further from the truth.

clear that illicit sex belongs in the same category of danger. Both inward and outward purity are vital for our spiritual and emotional health. The Patriarch Joseph knew how to escape sin quickly when Potiphar's wife tried to seduce him (see Gen. 39:11–12).

Evading general sexual sin is one thing, but what about the premarital kind? Some argue that since neither Hebrew nor Greek have a specific word for "premarital sex" between two unmarried partners, it is not addressed in the Bible. That couldn't be further from the truth. In the New Testament, the Greek word *porneía* is a term used for a range of immoralities, including "seduction, rape, sodomy, bestiality, certain forms of incest, prostitution (male or female), and homosexual relations."[6] But it's also used to describe any type of "illegal sexual intercourse" outside of a marriage, "except that between a husband and wife."[7] Scholar Ben Witherington III clearly asserts, "*Porneia* can refer to all sorts of sexual sin including deflowering a virgin."[8] Thus, when the apostle Paul commanded the church to "abstain from sexual immorality" (1 Thess. 4:3), he meant to stay away from *all* of the sexual sins listed above, including fornication.

Also take into account that, in biblical times, virgins were highly valued. Witherington further explains, "In early Jewish law if you had sex with a woman you were considered married to her or you had shamed her."[9] In essence, to be involved sexually *meant* you were married. If a man seduced a virgin before he married her, at the very least he had to pay a fine. Consider the potential penalty imposed in Exodus 22:16–17:

> If a man seduces a virgin who is not engaged, and lies with her, he must pay a dowry for her to be his wife. If her father absolutely refuses to give her to him, he shall pay money equal to the dowry for virgins. (NASB 1995)

Marriage wasn't a foregone conclusion after the man's sin. For one reason, an angry father was involved (the English Standard Version says, "utterly refuses"). Why would he be upset if this man had acted honorably toward his daughter? Professor Bill T. Arnold notes that the man who violated the woman had "gotten the process reversed. He should have negotiated the bride-price, then married her, then had intercourse. . . . [The man] has willfully done something wrong and must now make amends."[10]

The New Testament is just as clear. A big portion of what it means to be "holy" or "set apart" for God comes from what we do with our bodies. First Thessalonians 4:3–5 states, "This is the will of God, your sanctification; that is, that you abstain from sexual immorality; that each of you know how to possess his own vessel in sanctification and honor, not in lustful passion, like the Gentiles who do not know God." Pertaining to this passage, Fredrick J. Long, professor of New Testament and director of Greek instruction at Asbury Theological Seminary, observed, "His will is defined as 'holiness' and this holiness is immediately specified in terms of avoiding sexual immorality."[11] In other words, Paul swiftly attached God's will to holiness and sexual purity.

Many ask, *What is God's will for my life?* You may have taken a spiritual gifts assessment or a job placement test to find out how you can assimilate your passions and skill set into the perfect job or ministry. Yet, in all the ways you search for your calling, God describes it here in terms of being "holy" and avoiding "sexual immorality." The New Living Translation is straightforward: "God's will is for you to be holy, so stay away from all sexual sin" (1 Thess. 4:3).

Then we are left with the words of Jesus: "I say to you that everyone who looks at a woman with lust for her has already committed adultery with her in his heart" (Matt. 5:28). This is the part where Jesus drops the mic and walks off the stage.

Be Careful with Super Glue

Science also alludes to how God designed our "attachment hormones" for marriage. Have you ever accidentally superglued two fingers together? Just one dab rapidly melds them, and pulling them apart causes severe pain. God wants you to wait for sexual activity because it is like a fast-acting super glue. It bonds people together quickly and rushes a relationship forward. Some physical expression in a dating relationship is appropriate. Yet I advocate that *any* kind of physical touch in dating too soon puts your heart at risk. It also makes your head cloudy and distracts you from actually getting to know someone, the latter of which is the most important part in dating.

God not only designed our sexual organs but the associated chemical compounds as well. Romantic touch triggers your brain to release potent hormones like oxytocin, dopamine, norepinephrine, and vasopressin.[12] These produce lovely, feel-good, God-given emotions. What's important to remember is that this hormone cocktail already starts lighting up your brain even as you go on a new date or begin an exhilarating relationship. But physical touch and sex can stimulate them to the point where logic stops and feelings or hormones override your ability to make clear decisions. Not only are the levels of oxytocin already "significantly higher in new lovers compared to singles,"[13] but physical affection like "hugs, snuggles, kisses, and sex also activate more of it."[14]

You've probably heard of a starry-eyed couple who met, fell in love, and couldn't keep their hands off each other. They rocketed from dating to exchanging impassioned "I love you's" to talking about marriage only a few weeks after meeting. They espoused romantic confessions like, "I know we just met, but I feel as if I've known you for years." They are always holding hands, making out, and gazing into each other's eyes. One confesses to her friend that they are involved sexually, but says, "God will forgive us, because we're planning to get married." They are engaged for a short time when suddenly the whirlwind relationship grinds to a halt. A terrible breakup ensues. Each person separately admits their relationship escalated way too quickly.

What was that? How could a couple be head-over-heels one minute then break up the next? An intoxicating elixir of emotion and infatuation drove their relationship, not God. Oxytocin has been dubbed the "love hormone" or the "cuddling hormone," because it's associated with feelings of closeness, trust, and attachment.[15] According to the Harvard Mahoney Neuroscience Institute, oxytocin is "released during sex and heightened by skin-to-skin contact," which makes couples feel closer and stay together.[16]

The problem is, these chemicals aren't inert. In one telling study, researchers in Switzerland investigated the effects of oxytocin by testing it on a group of participants. One group was administered a dose of it via a nasal spray, while another control group was given a placebo. Both were then presented with an opportunity to invest money in a potentially shady business deal. Here's the scary part: the people who had taken the oxytocin were more likely to trust the presenter and give more of their money away without the possibility of ever receiving a return.[17] Relating this study to dating, marriage and family therapist Stacy Hubbard notes that with elevated levels of oxytocin, "you are less likely to notice risk and more likely to make poor decisions."[18] Oxytocin, along with its chemical relatives, dopamine and serotonin, make you feel floaty and infatuated.[19] It's inevitable that you'll already be drinking some of this powerful euphoric mixture just by being in an exciting dating relationship. Enjoy them. At the same time, be careful about stoking them into an inferno through excessive physical touch. Also, don't equate them with trusting the person. Powerful emotions can burn you. Overstimulating their production will hinder your logical brain and blind you to any red flags God is trying to show you about your boyfriend or girlfriend.

C. S. Lewis stated that "indulgence brings fog."[20] If your girlfriend or boyfriend has money problems, anger issues, addictions, or any other severe issue, intense physical touch, sex, and even kissing will cloud your judgment. Worse, you won't even know you're foggy. Even if you have decided that you like them for the right reasons, raging hormones can distract you from actually getting to know them. What you need in dating is clarity and a level head. Simply put, what you need to know about a potential mate won't be found by making out or rounding second or third base. You need to discover their likes, dislikes, hopes, dreams, and faith in Christ. The salient questions you'll want to answer are, "Do you share the same core values?" "Do you have fun together?" and "Could you serve God greater together?" not "Are you a good kisser?"

Sexual pleasure and romantic physical touch fire so many feel-good chemicals in your brain that you may believe you "fell in love," but in reality, you only fell into a feeling. Regardless of what the movies say, vows need to be exchanged from volition, not passion. Therefore, make it to the altar through a clear thought process. After the covenant is formed, you can act on and fully release those wonderful chemicals in all their glory.

With such a high divorce rate, why risk tainting the decision-making process by going too far physically? Learn to "wait well" for sex. Otherwise, you'll be forced to bear the consequences of dishonoring God, trusting someone too soon, making poorer choices, risking getting your heart crushed, and leaving a broken relationship with regret.

How to Wait Well

When I was on holiday in Turkey, during a short stay at a hostel, I met three college-aged, nonreligious guys from different Western countries. After an hour of sipping Turkish tea together and talking about travel, one of them asked how I came to faith in Christ. I explained how I didn't grow up following Jesus. But during my time at my university, God began working in my heart. I told them about my profound spiritual conversion at age twenty-one. I also mentioned that I recommitted to not have sex until marriage. Their jaws dropped. With incredulity, one said, "How can you wait? Is that even possible? Isn't that against nature?" They acted as if they'd die without sex. (For the record, as my friend quipped, "No one ever died from not having sex.")

As Christians, we aren't immune to the onslaught of sexual temptation. But we also have the advantage of being empowered through the Holy Spirit: "For God has not given us a spirit of timidity, but of power and love and discipline" (2 Tim. 1:7). Our job is to open the spiritual valve and allow Him to lead and shape our sexuality. Many Christians have tried to honor God with their bodies but haven't yet arranged a kind of life where both purity of heart and sexual purity are experienced. As G. K. Chesterton said, "The Christian ideal has not been tried and found wanting. It has been found difficult; and left untried."[21] What will you cultivate in order to align your heart to God and keep sex in the rightful place? The opposite of sexual sin isn't abstinence but a wholeheartedness to Christ.

If you have questions about the grace-giving practices that form our character to Christ's, I refer you back to chapter 5. There we discussed the practices that connect us to God, such as reading the Bible, praying, and finding a trustworthy mentor. But let's review a few highlights specific to the topic of sex.

Memorizing Scripture is vital in replacing sexual images and fantasies. With a sex-everywhere culture, most of our brains need at least some reprogramming. As I previously mentioned, I've written dozens of Bible verses on index cards. I keep them by my bed and read them before I sleep. The more I recite them, the more my mind is filled with Scripture. One of them is Romans 12:1–2:

> I urge you, brothers and sisters, by the mercies of God, to present your bodies a living and holy sacrifice, acceptable to God, which is your spiritual service of worship. And do not be conformed to this world, but be transformed by the renewing of your mind, so that you may prove what the will of God is, that which is good and acceptable and perfect.

Fasting is another spiritual avenue in learning how to say no to your body's cravings. As you deny satisfying your urge to eat, you're training yourself to say no to impulsive sexual feelings. If you're dating and struggling with sexual activity, practice a full day of fasting with your boyfriend or girlfriend, specifically to train yourselves to save sex for marriage. To make it more effective, meet with a mentor beforehand and have them join you in prayer for this time. Ask God to empower your outward activity of going without food so that you can say no to sex until marriage, and yes to appropriate physical touch in dating.

As you pray, beseech God for a spirit of self-control. The Greek word for "self-control" as listed in Galatians 5:23 is *enkatreia*. It means to be in charge of yourself or "having power in oneself."[22] Begin with your speech. As James says, "If we could control our tongues, we would be perfect and could also control ourselves in every other way" (3:2 NLT). Get your speech in order and you'll also be ordering your sexuality. Crass humor, swapping fantasies, and lionizing past sexual exploits will only stir up that part of you that wants to act outside of God's limits. Instead, practice "singing psalms and hymns and spiritual songs among yourselves, and making music to the Lord in your hearts" (Eph. 5:19 NLT).

Mentoring other people has sharply taught me about controlling my own sexuality. For five years, I was a "big brother" to a young man who was experiencing the raging teenage hormones. We'd get together once or twice a month, and I'd have to correct his catcalls toward women and his sexual innuendos. I taught him about God and sex, differentiating between love and lust. The invaluable benefit of mentoring is the conviction you feel when preaching one thing while struggling with the same thing. If that special dagger of hypocrisy isn't a catalyst for change, I don't know what is. My goal was to help him become a young man of God, but I wonder if he taught me more than I ever taught him. Find a younger man or woman to pour into and the Lord will change *you* in the process.

Other than spiritual disciplines, here are some additional practical tips. Keeping a full schedule as you date also helps in your fight against temptation. Instead of staying home with your boyfriend or girlfriend, go out and get some physical exercise together. It will keep you in shape and you'll get a natural release of dopamine. Take a stroll in a park, tackle a trail run, register for a painting class, or attend a lecture on a topic new to you both. Avoid sitting around for endless hours streaming movies. Stay busy with any of the ten-thousand activities that help you avoid spending time in each other's apartments alone. Hang out with other people as a couple and date in groups.

The final way to "wait well" is to stop waiting. Have you been dating for five years, developed a stable, life-giving relationship, and feel ants in your pants? As my good business friend says, "Seal the deal." Get married. As Paul says, "If they do not have self-control, let them marry; for it is better to marry than to burn with passion" (1 Cor. 7:9). One of the problems with singles waiting longer than ever to get married is that their passions are on fire for much longer than their predecessors. Of course, you'd never marry just to have sex, but it can be an added motivator.

What Can You Do in Dating?

I've deliberately left this section to the end because I didn't want you to get caught up in the "how far is too far" argument. Illicit sex is powerful enough to ruin your reputation, your well-being, and your relationship. Therefore, be proactive in creating boundaries around your sexuality. Within these limits and in the time before marriage, I'd advise you not to engage in activities beyond holding hands, putting your arms around each other, and giving simple kisses on the lips. Long embraces, horizontally cuddling on the couch, making out, and naps together are best saved until after the wedding bells. As you wrote a list of key events in chapter 6, write down the type of physical affections you're comfortable showing at each stage of the relationship. Examine your heart and make decisions based on your devotion to Christ, faithfulness to Scripture, and Spirit-guided conscience.

God loves sex because He created it. He also loves you. That's why He wants you to be careful with your sexual organs. Celibacy is only possible if it starts on the inside. True purity is a wholeheartedness toward God. If you've messed up as I have in the past, rest in the fact that "we do not have a high priest who cannot sympathize with our weaknesses, but One who has been tempted in all things just as we are, yet without sin" (Heb. 4:15). Savor the emotional buzz of romance but stay within God's limits of physical touch. Otherwise, you risk letting a powerful hormonal brew cloud your judgment and distract you from getting to know the person. The key to sexual purity is growing in your character and becoming more like Christ. Staying close to God will give you a clear conscience and prepare you to experience a guilt-free, fulfilling, and God-honoring sex life in marriage.

CHAPTER 10

Getting the Best from a Breakup

"Behold, I am doing a new thing; now it springs forth, do you not perceive it? I will make a way in the wilderness and rivers in the desert."
—Isaiah 43:19 ESV

I was thirteen and arrived at school a few minutes before 8:00 a.m. Suddenly, my girlfriend's best friend walked straight up to me on the asphalt playground, took me aside, and gushed, "Amy wants to break up with you. You know why, right?" I was taken aback but wanted to play it cool. Nodding with confidence, I responded, "Yeah, I know why." And that was that—it was over. I didn't have a clue why my girlfriend wanted to break up. I couldn't bring myself to ask. Today, I still don't know the reason.

It's easy to snicker at junior high drama. But after dating in my adult years, I have experienced the excruciating pain at the end of a serious relationship. Whether we land on the giving or receiving end, our heart sinks at these comments and the reality behind them:

"We need to end our relationship."
"I see us only being friends."
"We're not compatible."
"My heart isn't in this anymore."
"I don't see this going to marriage."

Maybe prescience told you that the relationship was doomed, but you needed to hear it to make it official. Or maybe the breakup was a bombshell. In either case, ending a romance can feel as if someone dropped a piano on your heart.

I experienced the fallout of a broken engagement and know that that kind of pain is enough for one lifetime. Letting go, healing, and moving forward was a snail-like process. I felt like King David in Psalm 143: "Therefore my spirit is overwhelmed within me" (v. 4 NKJV). I can't imagine how devastating a divorce would feel—and don't want to.

We've discussed how relationships begin, and we can't ignore that they may end. Numerous gems are waiting to be mined in the depths of despair. God doesn't waste pain. The Lord uses suffering to grow character, make us more like Him, and prepare us for our next relationship that will hopefully go the distance. Traits like perseverance, tenacity, faith, and utter dependence on Christ are forged in the fire of our pain.

How do you get the best from a breakup?

Get Feedback and Grow

Many parents encourage their children to "try, try again" as they learn how to ride a bike or tie their shoes, but it's unwise to apply this principle in relationships. You need time to heal. If you side-step the healing process and rebound too quickly, you won't have space to learn what to do better the next time. If a three-hundred-million-dollar rocket exploded in midair, NASA wouldn't say, "Let's try another launch tomorrow."[1] The scientists would analyze what went wrong, complete a damage report, modify the rocket design, then send up a safer rocket. Use the interim between relationships to conduct a sober assessment of yourself. Ask, "What can I do better next time?" and "How can I be more prepared for my next relationship?"

Let the Holy Spirit guide you, and pray Psalm 139:23–24:

Search me, O God, and know my heart;
Put me to the test and know my anxious thoughts;
And see if there is any hurtful way in me,
And lead me in the everlasting way.

Be a student of yourself. If you notice you come on too strong or desperate and scare potential mates away, practice becoming tactful, patient, and gentle with your approach. If you've been too passive in making your needs known to your partner, learn asser-tiveness. Some singles discover they were so focused on finding someone with a perfect body that they forgot about character and godliness. If you've experienced multiple breakups, see if you can detect an unhealthy pattern in yourself or the type of person you keep choosing. For example, it's not uncommon for people to get stuck dating their opposites. Often, however, talkers get frustrated with taciturns, the poised tire of pixies, and extroverts nag their introverted boyfriend or girlfriend to socialize more. The wear-your-heart-on-your-sleeves type might unknowingly always choose the mysterious ones. Of course, all these different relationship combinations can work in dating and marriage. My only point is that if insanity is defined as doing the same thing over and over again and expecting different results, try dating someone different.

The next way to grow is to ask for feedback. Blind spots, by definition, mean we don't know what to work on. We need help.

If you don't ask, how will you know? I found the moxie after one relationship ended to directly ask the woman I was involved with how I could improve. Indeed, it was scary, but what she said was helpful. I learned from my mistakes and inched closer to becoming more like Christ. Although you might want to forget someone as soon as possible after a breakup, men and women from previous relationships are invaluable resources for gaining maturity.

If asking a previous partner is too intense, get feedback from a trusted friend or family member. Ask them if they notice any glaring issues or patterns you have that could negatively affect your dating. Even if they don't, find a close few to process your breakup with. Praying with friends and absorbing their unconditional love and acceptance will help you move forward.

Feedback is a lost art, but you needn't have any fear of receiving it. I'm not talking about self-condemnation or dwelling on your faults. Reflection isn't pathologizing yourself. You are "precious" in God's eyes, so be kind to yourself (Isa. 43:4). We all make mistakes—they are inherent to who we are. The playing field is leveled because we "all have sinned and fall short of the glory of God" (Rom. 3:23). I probably have an exclusive dating outtakes reel in heaven's archives.[2]

As you assess yourself and ask God and others, take a sober

approach but give yourself mercy and grace. As Paul tells us, "Don't think you are better than you really are. Be honest in your evaluation of yourselves, measuring yourselves by the faith God has given us" (Rom. 12:3 NLT).

A few rough edges in your habits or personality doesn't mean you caused the breakup. They also don't disqualify you from a meaningful relationship. But breakups are too painful to waste. Don't sweep the pain under the rug, because you'll trip over it later. Take the time to evaluate your actions, get feedback, and assess what you could do better next time.

Not Wise to Ask Whys

As someone said, God doesn't answer our why questions; instead, He gives us promises. While receiving feedback and learning from mistakes mitigates risk, it will never eliminate it. It's often impossible to know precisely *why* a relationship didn't work out. A blatant sin issue like cheating, addiction, or deceit presents a clear answer, but many times the cause is simply a waning heart. The desire to date disintegrates, and you lose hope that the relationship will make it to marriage.

As we discussed previously, the reason two people come together and form a stunning purple is a mystery. But it's the same when hearts fade and two people sense it's just not going to work out. All the ingredients for a great relationship might have been there, but you or your partner disagreed. I think it's true when people say, "You'll know when you know that you want to marry someone." I also believe the converse holds: you know that it's a no.

I believe God protected me from pain down the road by keeping me unmarried up to this point. It reminds me of the Garth Brooks song "Unanswered Prayers." In the lyrics, Brooks thanks God for not answering his prayers to be with a former flame because of his current happiness with his wife. We must trust that God knows what is best for us in the long term. As Timothy Keller notes:

> God gives you what you would have asked for if you knew everything he knows. If we knew everything God knew, therefore what he was giving me; he actually always answered your prayers. Yet, he finds different ways to answer prayers. When we pray we give what we want. God says look I will give you but not the way you want.[3]

The key is to do everything you can to be the person you want to be with and not to get stuck asking the why questions. Instead, keep your eyes open for how God wants to shape you through a relationship or a breakup.

How to End It

I was leaving church and noticed the despondent look on a woman's face as she checked her phone. Her boyfriend had just broken up with her over a text. Stunned, she murmured, "He couldn't even call?" My heart still hurts when I picture her face.

When you've come to an end for a relationship, communicate with honor, love, and respect. There are different ways you can convey your decision:

Texting/Emails → Phone Calls → Video Calls → In-Person Meetings

Starting from the left, texting and emailing are the least personal, phone calls and video calls are more personal, and in-person meetings are the most personal. The words you use to break up are important, but not nearly as much as *how* you go about doing it. Most meaningful are your facial expressions, gestures, body language, and vocal inflection. A poignant text might have all the right words, but it will come across as blithe and detached, because your partner won't receive the emotion behind it.

The method of breakup should be determined by the stage of your relationship. If you've had one nonexclusive date, you may not need to say anything at all (unless you said you would), or you could send a quick message saying, "Thank you. I had a wonderful time getting to know you, but I'm not interested in taking things further." Context is key. If that same first date was scheduled after several long, online conversations over the span of a month, then you owe the person at least a follow-up message but probably a short phone call. Similarly, if you were in a more intimate stage, such as an exclusive relationship, that person deserves at least an extended phone call and probably an in-person meeting. Furthermore, ending a serious relationship or breaking an engagement would require at least one in-person conversation and likely follow-up conversations. Video calling helps if it's a long-distance relationship. Whatever you do, don't just stop communicating with someone with whom you have been in regular contact.

In addition to determining your communication method based on the stage of your relationship, there are two more principles to follow when initiating a breakup. One is if you can't decide between two ways of ending it, do the more personal one. Often, the hardest option is the godliest and most respectful (remember, go toward what is USA—uncomfortable, scary, and awkward). The caveat to this principle is that if you're ending a relationship because of its abusive nature, then clearly it would not be wise to meet in person. The other is if you're in doubt, follow the Golden Rule: "Do unto others as you would have them do unto you." Put yourself in your partner's shoes. How would you want to hear it? If you're eager to say, "I'd be okay with a text if someone wanted to break up," then consider what might happen when you see them next. It's much less awkward to see an ex-boyfriend or girlfriend if you broke up over a phone call or in person rather than through a text.

Even though a relationship doesn't go to marriage, you can still bless someone with the gift of a respectful breakup. Flowers can be found in the fallout. The choice is yours—do you want them to remember your sourness or civility? Your guilt trip or gratitude for your time together? As far as it depends on you, exit a relationship as you'd want someone else to. This includes honesty, honor, and care. As difficult as they are, healthy breakups will help you and the other person heal faster, remain unharmed, and be ready for the next relationship. The bottom line is that if you can't end a relationship well, you're not ready to start one.

Staying with your boyfriend or girlfriend is always your choice. You always have a right to walk away. Don't hang on to a wrong relationship out of obligation, because "God told you," or because other people believe he or she is an excellent fit. If you had sex, but also know you don't want to marry this person, don't stay with them based on guilt or an emotional attachment. God will forgive you for going too far physically, and He'd never force you to marry someone you didn't want to. Deep down, we often know what's best for us but sometimes have a hard time letting go.

Finally, if there's physical, emotional, or sexual abuse in the relationship, that's instant grounds for a breakup. Similarly, if there's a pattern of manipulation, it's time to call it quits. Even if you're in love, or you believe, *This person will change someday*, God loves you too much to see you experience that kind of treatment.

Likewise, though your family and friends have good intentions and want to see you happy and married, in the end you—and you alone—will bear the consequences of staying in a relationship and getting married. Your family won't be waking up next to that person each morning. Your best friend won't be taking care of your spouse when he or she gets old. You will be. You also don't need a Scripture verse to back up your reason to end a dating relationship or engagement. If your heart isn't in it, you can walk away without judging yourself or feeling guilty. He or she might be an amazing person, but not *your* amazing man or woman. Even if you're sexually attracted to them and like them as a person, you still may not want to be in a relationship with them. One of the most mature traits you can develop is the ability to restrain yourself from dating someone even though you're highly attracted to them.

If they are a gem and it was a tough decision to end it, say that it was an honor to date them.

How to Heal a Broken Heart and Have Hope Again

In the children's book *We're Going on a Bear Hunt*, an adventurous family encounters several obstacles in their journey, including "oozy mud," a "swirling whirling snowstorm," and a "big, dark forest."[4] At every hurdle, they repeat this mantra:

> We can't go over it.
> We can't go under it.
> Oh no!
> We've got to go through it!

Indeed, we have no shortcuts to healing a broken heart. We must go through it. The pain can't be minimized, medicated, or mollified. We need to feel it.

I've struggled extensively with pain from scuttled relationships. They are big pills to swallow knowing that one hasn't worked out yet and that I'll be an older husband and (maybe) an older father. Going through it means that we allow ourselves to grieve and feel the loss.

Struggling emotionally doesn't mean you are a second-class Christian. It means you're authentic. After a breakup, it's appropriate to simultaneously experience grief and hold onto the hope found in Christ. Jesus was fully man and experienced every human emotion. The shortest verse the Bible is also one of the most profound: "Jesus wept" (John 11:35). He's not just looking down on your pain but is *with you* in the grief: "The Lord is near to the brokenhearted and saves those who are crushed in spirit" (Ps. 34:18).

> You know you've genuinely forgiven someone and healed from a relationship when you can look back, have peace in your heart, and truly bless your previous boyfriend or girlfriend.

Everyone handles pain and suffering differently. If you've had a recent breakup, you might want to talk about it, not talk about it, punch a pillow, jog every day, or journal ten pages in one sitting as I once did. I've made so many altar calls crying out to God that I've lost count. Maybe I'm a sucker for punishment, but as my mentor revealed, "Eric, God uses relationships to keep you on your knees in prayer." Does He do the same for you?

You can take steps to move forward and heal faster. If you have pictures, notes, cards, or gifts that painfully remind you of your relationship, get rid of them. You don't need memorabilia to remember how you felt about someone. You'll have to decide when to let these keepsakes go. My friend took a pile of his notes and set them aflame as a cathartic action of emotional release. Staying busy with family and friends also helps. Call people and go out to eat, rent motorcycles, or go on a road trip together. You could start a new class, join a gym, or take up a new hobby. Keep your mind on other things rather than your previous boyfriend or girlfriend. The point is to distract your mind and replace the thoughts of your ex with new memories and joyful experiences. When a thought pops up about them and you feel the loss again, validate your grief, but then refocus.

I recommend avoiding the person you dated for a while if your heart was broken. Taking a break from places you know they will be will bring faster healing. Dodging the person doesn't make you weak; it makes you wise. Set up boundaries with your friends by asking them to refrain from relaying new info to you about your ex—like the new person he or she is dating. When you want to know how they are, you'll be the one to ask.

Forgiveness is paramount to completing the healing process —both for yourself and for the other person. Forgiveness is a "term used to indicate pardon for a fault or offense; to excuse from payment for a debt owed."[5] If someone harmed you, forgiveness doesn't mean you forgot what happened; instead, you allow God to administer the consequences. Forgiveness heals your heart by removing any contempt, anger, or desire for retaliation. As one chaplain noted, "Forgiveness does not mean friendship."[6] It's realizing the same blood that covers your sins covers theirs. Jesus was serious when He said, "If you do not forgive other people, then your Father will not forgive your offenses" (Matt. 6:15). You know you've genuinely forgiven someone and healed from a relationship when you can look back, have peace in your heart, and truly bless your previous boyfriend or girlfriend.

If you made mistakes during the relationship, let them go. All mistakes aren't sins, but all sins are mistakes. For the egregious kind, look at yourself in the mirror, say what you did wrong, and ask God to forgive you. Then, while still looking in the mirror, say, "I forgive myself." After that, release it. You can then outline a circle with your hands in the shape of a balloon and lift it up to God as a representation of letting go of sin, pain, or worry. If you can't forgive yourself alone, invite a trusted friend, therapist, or pastor to help you. If you need to contact your ex and ask for forgiveness for a specific grievance you caused, pray about it, then sit on it for at least a week. Once you know your motives are pure, then write an email.

I don't believe time heals all wounds because I've met plenty of bitter people who've held onto past sins for decades. The truth is, over time, and with God's help, we can heal. But it's a process. As you stay busy with friends, pray, journal, and get counsel, light will start shining through the darkness of despair. You'll have gaps in your pain and begin experiencing joy again. The gaps between grief will become bigger and bigger, and before you know it, you'll be thinking of them less and less. One day you'll wake up and realize that joy is the new norm, and you're "over" them.

Will You Get Back Together?

If a relationship didn't work the first time, chances are it won't work the next. I'm not here to tell you if you will or won't get back together with someone you loved. God can do anything. One couple I heard of broke up ten times before they were married. Rekindling an old flame isn't out of the realm of possibility, but you need to let go of the relationship and all emotional attachment before you can start anything new. Only the Lord knows what the future holds. Accepting reality will help you reset and move forward.

Some people get caught in a pattern of wishful thinking or calling down specific promises from heaven for their love life. Reality is unyielding against wishful thinking and fantasies. Dallas Willard defines reality as "what you run into when you're wrong."[7] If your boyfriend or girlfriend said no, believe them. Let them go. They know how to get in touch with you if they change their mind.

Similarly, "missing" someone is not a good reason to contact a former partner or get back together. Missing someone—feeling the loss of his or her presence—is normal and shows you invested in the relationship. If you didn't miss them, you didn't care. Here's a good reason to get back together: both of you want to be with each other. You have taken time apart, grown, and now can form a dish both of you enjoy. Whatever happens, don't bypass the normal grieving process and get back together too quickly.

If you've had six months apart and the man or woman is still on your heart, consider contacting them. Before you do, answer this crucial question: What would be different? If the relationship didn't work the first time, something needs to change to make it work the second round. If you can't provide a thorough answer, you're likely headed for another painful breakup. But if you recognized an unhealthy pattern in your own life and have changed, if the other person changed in some way, or if outside circumstances changed, then type that message or pick up the phone and see where it leads.

When to Date Again

When you've learned from your last breakup, are free of its pain, have forgiven, and hope has returned—that's when you can date again. If you're still in emotional recovery and start dating, you'll morph into that vacuum cleaner and start taking from someone new. Some singles are ready to date after a couple weeks, while others need months or years to heal. The length and magnitude of your pain is entirely personal and depends on what stage you were in when the relationship ended. If it stopped at engagement, you might need months before another date. If you broke up after a few dates, you could be ready next weekend. I've heard people make the rule that the length of time you dated is the same amount of time you need to wait before starting your next relationship. I disagree—people recover and move forward at different speeds.

Another indication to know if you're ready is when another breakup won't crush you. If you fear it or couldn't bear to go through another one, then take more time to heal.

Finally, be careful when you start dating again, because you'll automatically gravitate toward the stage where your previous relationship ended. For example, if your last relationship ended at the serious exclusive stage, you'll be tempted to get back to this stage ASAP. Likewise, if you were engaged, watch that you don't quickly form another serious commitment too soon. Take your time. (The opposite can also be true—you were so hurt from a broken engagement that now you are wary of another serious relationship.)

If you experienced a breakup, stay encouraged. Proverbs 4:25 states, "Let your eyes look directly ahead and let your gaze be fixed straight in front of you." Remember that it only takes one right relationship to get to marriage.

God may not give you answers to why a relationship didn't work out, but that doesn't mean a fantastic redemptive story isn't in the making. Get the best out of a breakup. Find healing, learn from it, and come out a better person with a stronger faith in God. Thank Him now—even when you don't feel like it—for unanswered prayers.

CHAPTER 11

Fall in Love with Your Cheesecake

The greatest thing you and I can imagine is the fellowship of other loving persons, to love and to be loved, to know, to enjoy, to be with, to adventure, to create.
—DALLAS WILLARD, *LIFE WITHOUT LACK*

Baking is a fascinating phenomenon. Eating eggs, flour, sugar, butter, and graham crackers by themselves isn't tasty. Mix them together and put the concoction in the oven for an hour, however, and a delicious cheesecake magically appears. Baking a cheesecake is like forming a relationship—two people come together and bring their values, preferences, personalities, and belief systems and develop something new—a "third thing." But why some people go well together and others don't is a mystery. A man and woman who are similar and meet each other's long list of nonnegotiables doesn't guarantee they will enjoy the "third thing" created when they start dating. In contrast, couples who don't perfectly align on paper still might create a surprisingly long and life-giving marriage.

For example, Sam and Suzi have been dating six months. The middle section of their Venn diagram below represents what Sam and Suzi are forming between them—their relationship "cheesecake." As Suzi dates Sam for the possibility of marriage, she must now evaluate their relationship patterns as a whole just as much as she's evaluating his specific traits. Initially, Suzi was attracted to Sam's "hotness," commitment to Christ, and desire to have lots of kids—the same values she shares. Now Suzi needs to ask herself questions like, *Do I enjoy spending time with him, or am I only sexually attracted to him? Is our relationship a safe place to disagree or do we walk on eggshells around each other? Can I be myself with him?* In other words, Suzi is determining not only if she loves Sam but if she loves her relationship with him. Likewise, she's not only deciding whether she wants to marry Sam but if she wants to marry their relationship.

Look at the diagram this way: when you marry, not only will you live with another person, you'll live with how you relate to each other (that's why it's called a "relate-tionship"). It's these patterns of interactions that form your cheesecake and define the relationship—from how you greet each other in the morning, to how you manage stressful situations as a couple, to the ways you relax together on a Sunday afternoon. Some combinations will taste good and bring you joy, while others will be bitter or blasé. With this insight in mind, here are three keys in understanding your "cheesecake."

Not All Ingredients Taste Good Together

The first key to understanding your cheesecake is that people are like ingredients—not all of them taste good when mixed together. I love ketchup on my hamburger and wasabi on my sushi, but I wouldn't douse my tuna rolls in Heinz.[1] Ketchup and wasabi only complement certain foods. Likewise, some otherwise great people don't go well together when you combine them; they will form a mismatched relationship. Just because Sam is a "great guy" and fulfills everything on Suzi's nonnegotiable list doesn't mean that he and Suzi will form a sweet and delicious relationship. In the same way, it's a dating myth that two Christ followers will automatically go well together. Faith is the foundation, but much more on top of that needs to mesh.

After college, I dated a woman for several months but was unsure about marrying her. Our nonnegotiables lined up as we were both new Christians, had a love for the lost, enjoyed the outdoors, and felt a sizzling attraction toward each other. In theory, we seemed a good match. But something in our recipe wasn't right. We fought constantly. I kept trying to force it to work, and we got stuck in that painful cycle of breaking up and getting back together again.

I didn't like who I was with her, and she didn't like who she was with me. We couldn't act as our true selves. To maintain harmony, we had to show up as different people when we were together. We wondered, *Why is this relationship so hard?* and *Why is this so much work?* I called my mentor and tried to convince him how I thought marriage would help us come together as a couple.

"Tim, won't God bless our marriage? We both love Jesus."

"Eric, do you like to gamble?"

"It depends."

"That's exactly what you're doing. You're gambling. God might ultimately bless your relationship, or He might not. But I'm certain marriage won't fix the problems you're both dealing with now. Take three months, work on your issues, and decide then."

But I kept pushing the marriage issue.

Finally, he said something I'll never forget: "Don't make me do divorce counseling on you."

Tim was right. God wasn't obligated to transform our unhappy dating relationship into a happy marriage, even though we both loved Him. I needed to step back and candidly look at how we related to each other. Fortunately, we didn't marry.

Incompatible People Can Work Well Together

The second observation is that some seemingly incompatible people work well together. I'm not talking about intractable differences in nonnegotiable values, I'm referring to discrepancies that seem like a big deal when you start dating but don't matter in the long-term. Let me illustrate with another food example. I never thought I'd like dipping McDonald's french fries into a chocolate shake, but when I did, I loved it. Others I know enjoy the sweet and salty combination too. The same goes for seemingly stark differences in people who get married. Even if you were raised in the inner city and they grew up in the suburbs, you have different skin colors, or you hold varying political views, don't let those differences stop you from dating— you could form something beautiful together.

I felt refreshed to hear about a woman who explained that she didn't marry her best friend. He wasn't her long-lost twin. She was chatty, and he was quiet. She was messy, but he was organized. For vacations, her husband liked hiking adventures in the mountains while she preferred a blissful bed at the Hilton. But they were convinced they were perfect for each other.

> Here is a bold prayer to pray: "Lord, give me the person I need, not the person I want."

God is a Creator who loves to bring two secure, strong, different people together to build something new and wonderful.

If you're waiting to meet someone who is the same as you, you might miss the person God actually wants to put in your path. God didn't intend for you to marry you. What's the fun in that? The Lord likes to create new things. As my mentor taught me, relationships are like the color purple—this regal shade is only created through a combination of blue and red. Look at the second chapter in Genesis: "For this reason a man shall leave his father and his mother, and be joined to his wife; and they shall become one flesh" (v. 24). Two become one and also form something new that the world has never seen.

When evaluating a potential spouse, it's vital to seek similarities, not sameness. To have a great relationship, you need to find common core values but not a person who is a clone. Marriage is about unity, not uniformity. Here is a bold prayer to pray: "Lord, give me the person I need, not the person I want." God might want you to partner with someone outside of your comfort zone. Purple is gorgeous, but it's only created by combining separate hues. To form your own exquisite orange or glittering green relationship, you might have to take a risk and go out with someone who is outside of your norm and very different than you.

Compatibility and Complementarity Are Not the Same

The third key to understanding your cheesecake is that you'll only know if it will be sweet or sour by spending a good chunk of time together and working on your relationship. Don't sprint to the emergency exit if you become alarmed that your partner values serving in the military while you believe war is an anathema. Similarly, if you want to move to another state, but they want to live near a dying grandparent, stay levelheaded. Many other couples have surmounted obstacles like these. God knows you're not the first couple to stand at a crossroads.

Start by inviting God into the situation, gaining His understanding, and yielding to His will. Trust that He is the One guiding the relationship. Pray Proverbs 3:5–6: "Trust in the LORD with all your heart; do not depend on your own understanding. Seek his will in all you do, and he will show you which path to take" (NLT).

Great relationships are not about finding compatibility but *complementarity*. Compatibility doesn't work in dating and marriage, because it means that something is inherently "designed to work with another device or system without modification."[2] It supports the false notions *I am who I am* and *I don't need to change.* Complementarity, on the other hand, is when someone "completes something" or "make it better."[3] We know God completes us, but it's true that our girlfriends, boyfriends, and future spouses can make us more like Him. One of the largest chemical companies in the world, BASF, had the slogan, "We don't make the products you buy; we make the products you buy better." Likewise, dating shouldn't create your spiritual life; it makes it better. In complementing each other, you'll both grow in godly traits like patience, perseverance, listening skills, and understanding different perspectives.

As G. K. Chesterton stated, "I cannot conceive why they are not all divorced. I have known many happy marriages, but never a compatible one. The whole aim of marriage is to fight through and survive the instant when incompatibility becomes unquestionable."[4] This quote is helpful for marriage, but it's not an exact rubric for dating. Dating doesn't have the same commitment level as marriage, so how hard you should work isn't entirely clear. In dating, you're giving the relationship enough breathing room for disagreements and differences while making sure it's not "too hard"—like in the case of the woman I dated after college. Over time you'll see if he or she is the right "wrong" one for you.

Evaluate Your Cheesecake

Now that you understand what a relationship is, how do you evaluate it? What are some common ingredients that make it nourishing and delicious? While each relationship will be unique, the healthy ones will share these foundational elements.

Healthy Conflict

As Max Lucado notes, "Conflict is inevitable, but combat is optional."[5] Miscommunication, disagreements, differences, and "not getting each other" are typical in dating. What is most important is not necessarily the specific topic you argue about but *how* you do it. By listening to each other's points, sharing your feelings, and seeking to understand your partner, you'll grow in mutual love and respect for each other even if you don't immediately solve the issue. Many people feel closer after an argument. (There's a reason the term *make-up sex* exists in marriage.)

Learning to love your partner even when you fight is imperative. The famous marriage researcher John Gottman measured with 91 percent accuracy whether couples would stay together or separate based on their fights. His amazingly precise prediction wasn't based on *if* they argue but *how*.[6] He named criticism, defensiveness, stonewalling, and contempt the *Four Horsemen of the Apocalypse*, where each one, respectively, is more deadly.[7] These responses in conflict are not only immature but toxic. They arise in the form of name-calling, justifying your actions, giving the silent treatment, disregarding what your partner has to say, and acting haughty and judgmental. The *coup de grâce* of the four horsemen is contempt, and it's "poisonous to a relationship because it conveys disgust."[8] If someone's poisonous attitude doesn't promptly change, the relationship is doomed.

Scripture has much to say on how to handle conflict:

- "A gentle answer turns away wrath, but a harsh word stirs up anger." (Prov. 15:1)
- "Death and life are in the power of the tongue, and those who love it will eat its fruit." (Prov. 18:21)
- "Blessed are the peacemakers, for they will be called sons of God. (Matt. 5:9)
- "If possible, so far as it depends on you, be at peace with all people." (Rom. 12:18)
- "Strive for full restoration, encourage one another, be of one mind, live in peace. And the God of love and peace will be with you." (2 Cor. 13:11 NIV)

- "Be angry, and yet do not sin." (Eph. 4:26)
- "Be kind to one another, compassionate, forgiving each other, just as God in Christ also has forgiven you." (Eph. 4:32)

Meditate on Bible verses like these. Incorporate them into your prayer life and study them with your boyfriend or girlfriend. If you're not in a relationship, practice what the Bible teaches about conflict with a cantankerous coworker, noisy roommate, or a sibling you butt heads with.

In addition, here are a few other practical tips for the next time you find yourself at odds with someone. When you share a grievance, begin conversations with "I" statements instead of "You" statements. Focus on your feelings and thoughts, withholding judgment of your partner. Say, "I feel upset that you arrived thirty minutes late for our date and didn't message me," not "Did another acute EMP blast-fry your smartwatch battery?" Likewise, try, "I am hurt that you didn't ask if I wanted to go" instead of "You never invite me to the monster truck races." (The words *always* and *never* are incendiary, so make sure you avoid them.)

When describing what made you upset, provide your version of the facts and listen to how your partner sees it. Don't judge someone's motivations or try to mind-read. If you become gridlocked in a seemingly intractable conflict—even one you believe isn't your fault—break the stalemate by finding at least one thing *you* could have done better and apologize for it. Owning at least part of the problem goes a long way toward reconciliation. Remember, "when pride comes, then comes dishonor; but with the humble there is wisdom" (Prov. 11:2). Taking a break to avoid a meltdown is wise during a fiery dialogue.

When you hurt your boyfriend or girlfriend's feelings, don't delay in saying, "I'm sorry" or "Please forgive me." Some people avoid these words when they believe they didn't do anything wrong, but just because you didn't intend for something to hurt doesn't make you inculpable. Apologize even for accidental pain your words or actions caused and ask how you could do it better next time. (Some people get hurt rather easily and require wisdom and grace to communicate with.) I've settled for the fact that I'll probably have to say, "I'm sorry" a million times in this life.

If you were the one offended, forgive quickly. I've read that people don't forgive because they fear they have something to lose by doing so. But you'll always "win" by forgiving, because you'll free yourself from the toxicity of stonewalling and contempt. In the international organization I work with, we have a saying: "Keep short accounts with one another." We teach our teams to let go of grievances swiftly and not harbor resentment. Jesus was emphatic about this idea: "If you forgive those who sin against you, your heavenly Father will forgive you. But if you refuse to forgive others, your Father will not forgive your sins" (Matt. 6:14–15 NLT).

Different Ways to Speak Love

Shakespeare wrote, "They do not love that do not show their love."[9] Indeed, love is a verb. It's impossible to say, "I love you" and truly mean it without putting it into practice. Dr. Gary Chapman's famous book *The 5 Love Languages®* lists various ways people give and receive love, including words of affirmation, acts of service, quality time, physical touch, and gifts. Knowing and incorporating each other's love language is crucial in understanding each other and showing love in a manner each can receive. Let's look briefly at the five.[10]

Words of affirmation include expressing with words the positive attributes of someone. People with this love language need notes, cards, verbal encouragement, and compliments. Hebrews 3:13 sums it up: "Encourage one another every day."

Acts of service is the language of help. It may include running errands for your partner, fixing their car, or assisting with a house project. Philippians 2:4 describes it: "Do not merely look out for your own personal interests, but also for the interests of others."

The third, *quality time*, is not the same as sitting in the same room or working on your laptop alongside him or her. It's intentional time set aside to talk or enjoy an activity together. Whatever you do, the focus is on the relationship, not necessarily on what you're doing. These people not only need a significant quantity of time but also importance in how that time is spent. The apostle Paul expressed this kind of deep desire in 1 Thessalonians: "In the same way we had a fond affection for you and were delighted to share with you not only the gospel of God, but also our own lives, because you had become very dear to us" (2:8).

In dating, the language of *physical (nonsexual) touch* can include putting your arm around your boyfriend or girlfriend, hugging, holding hands, and even light kissing. Although the Bible never discusses this topic among daters, we know that Jesus didn't shy away from physical endearment: "Jesus reached out with His hand and touched him, saying, 'I am willing; be cleansed.' And immediately his leprosy was cleansed" (Matt. 8:3).

Finally, people who receive love through *gifts* don't need offerings to be expensive, only thoughtful. A shell from the beach or a handmade card is often more appreciated than one from the store. You might pick up your partner's favorite cereal at the supermarket, buy a souvenir from an overseas trip, or send a surprise package in the mail. If Scripture shows that gifts were offered as a tribute, worship, dowry, and when people parted ways, then your special someone is worth them as well.[11]

On one of your dates, have fun and assess your and your partner's love languages. Find the free online tool on Chapman's website.[12] Spend time talking about your languages together.

As you practice love languages in dating, you'll become much more prepared for marriage. God delights in putting different people together, so you can bet that your girlfriend or boyfriend will have at least one distinct love language from yours. Chapman notes, "Seldom do a husband and wife have the same primary emotional love language."[13] One lady who recently married admitted to me that her husband appreciates gifts, but choosing one causes her angst. She could have practiced gift giving long before the wedding day. If a particular love language is difficult for you to express, get into the habit now. Dating is the perfect time to expand your ability to love in ways that may not be natural to you.

On a side note—if you are a guy, continue showing care and investment in your relationship with your girlfriend throughout each dating stage. Even when you have a solid commitment, most women value being pursued. Regularly ask her questions like, "Are you free Friday? I'd like to take you out on a date." I know how easy it is to fall into a rut of only hanging out and forgetting about special date nights. There's nothing wrong with doing daily life alongside your girlfriend, but plan at least one time per week where you go out for dinner, take a day trip to a neighboring city, or schedule a swing-dance lesson. If you're a woman, know that your man also likes it when you periodically plan a night out.

Communication and Listening Skills

Relationships need communication and listening skills to thrive. It doesn't matter if you're a Loquacious Lawrence or a Reserved Renee, it's important to consistently get to know your boyfriend or girlfriend. Dig into their life and find out about their likes and dislikes, family, pet peeves, and history. Stay curious about each other. Make sure the questions you ask are open-ended, prompting more interaction than just a "yes" or "no" response. Stacy Hubbard from the Gottman Institute explains, "Open-ended questions have stories for answers—and layers of meaning within those answers that can help you understand the heart of who your partner is."[14]

As you listen to your partner's answers, display an interest in what is going on in their world behind the scenes. Create time and space for conversations that reveal new things about each other. Consider asking lighter questions such as, "What's something you've won and how did you win it?" and deeper ones like, "What's weighing heavy on your heart these days?"[15] If you need other starters, *The Complete Book of Questions* by Garry Poole provides a thousand prompts.

Togetherness doesn't happen automatically. Your relationship will need two effective and active listeners. Active listening is more than hearing what someone said—it means you are physically, emotionally, and cognitively involved as the other person is sharing. Maintain eye contact, nod, and utter verbal cues—such as "Mmhm," "I hear you," "Tell me more," "That's great!"—to show that you're paying attention and are interested in what they are saying. Matching your emotion to your date will also connect you. The Bible says to "rejoice with those who rejoice, and weep with those who weep" (Rom. 12:15). When your partner is finished speaking, follow up with related open-ended questions. Inquire, but don't mine too deep in the beginning stages of dating.

In the previous chapters, we saw that one litmus test for whether you date someone is your curiosity level. Your curiosity not only shows that you might be interested in marriage, but also communicates how much you'd like to get to know a person. When curiosity is high, you inquire more—and it's a good sign. A lull in curiosity doesn't mean you need to break up; it probably only highlights that you're caught in a lazy spell.

Do You Like Yourself More?

Have you heard the phrase, *I lost myself in that relationship?* What people mean is that they couldn't act like themselves with the other person. It's hard to know why that happens—consistently not feeling yourself is probably a ketchup-and-sushi thing. But a sense of security and confidence in who you are is imperative in dating. In fact, the best girlfriends and boyfriends make each other feel *more* of who they were meant to be in Christ. Christian dating should bring out spiritual gifts and talents, and encourage each person to grow closer to God and move into his or her calling: "Encourage each other and build each other up, just as you are already doing" (1 Thess. 5:11 NLT).

A sense of foreboding shadows the relationship if you don't like yourself when you're with that person. My mentor shared a profound statement: "People don't break up because they don't like the other person but because they don't like *themselves* when they are with them." Heated disagreements are normal, but if you're overwhelmingly bringing out the best in each other, then that's a good sign the relationship is healthy and has potential for marriage.

You Get to Decide What You Form

Often people unconsciously recreate the same unhealthy relationship patterns they experienced growing up. It's not that they plan on it; human nature tends to reproduce whatever good, bad, or ugly patterns our parents modeled to us. Why? Research suggests that we gravitate toward repeating the kind of marriage that is familiar to us, even if it wasn't healthy. For example, one recent study on mothers found that the "number of maternal partners [she had] was positively associated with offspring's number of partners."[16] So if a mom had more cohabitating and marriage relationships, so did her children. Sociology researcher Claire Kamp Dush states, "What our results suggest is that mothers may pass on their marriageable characteristics and relationship skills to their children—for better or worse."[17]

Dush and other researchers know well that children whose parents divorced are more likely to divorce themselves.[18] Don't let that scare you aware from making a serious commitment, though. The good news is that even if you grew up with a distant father, alcoholic mother, abusive guardian, or divorced parents, you are not bound to mirror their mistakes. If your home life was amazing and two loving parents raised you, you are blessed indeed. Whatever the case, you can form healthier patterns for you and your future family. You are free to take the best from what you learned from your family and leave the rest. You, your partner, and God—not your past—are the ones who decide the kind of relationship you form. As Isaiah tells us in 43:18–19:

> "Do not call to mind the former things,
> Or consider things of the past.
> Behold, I am going to do something new,
> Now it will spring up;
> Will you not be aware of it?
> I will even make a roadway in the wilderness,
> Rivers in the desert."

And in the New Testament, Paul tells us, "Anyone who belongs to Christ has become a new person. The old life is gone; a new life has begun!" (2 Cor. 5:17 NLT).

If you need help shedding the past and learning more about what godly relationships entail, seek a Christian therapist or a trusted pastor to help. Also read relationship books by Gary Chapman, Timothy Keller, John Gottman, and Lysa TerKeurst.

There's no exact formula for why some people go well together and others don't. The best dating is a process of evaluating if you enjoy how you relate to each other. As you move through each stage, don't be surprised if it takes time and effort to discover whether you like what flavor of cheesecake you make as a couple. No matter who you date, you'll always discover differences. Measure the health of your relationship by how well you handle conflict, communicate, and serve each other. If you can be yourself with your boyfriend or girlfriend and if time passes by quickly when you're together, that's a good sign.

CHAPTER 12

You Found "The One" When You Can Love Like a Prince

And yet what they're looking for could be found in a single rose, or a little water.

—ANTOINE DE SAINT-EXUPÉRY, *THE LITTLE PRINCE*

In the famous book *The Little Prince*,[1] a prince discovers a unique seed on his planet and anxiously waits to see what sprouts. When the plant springs to life, a flower blooms, and he exclaims, "How lovely you are!" An exquisite rose stands before him; indeed, one that he's never seen before. It even speaks.

"Would you be so kind as to tend to me?" she asks.

Finding a watering can, he begins to care for the lovely new flower.

His kindness touches her as he dedicates himself to looking after the enchanting rose. Finally, the rose reveals her affection for him. "Of course, I love you," she tells him.

The Little Prince is smitten and believes he has the only rose in the universe.

After a crash landing on earth, the prince stumbles upon an entire bed of roses. He is shocked to see so many other roses who look just like his. The one he's been caring for was not one-of-a-kind after all. He laments that "five thousand of them" are "all just alike, in just one garden! . . . I thought I was rich because I had just one flower, and all I own now is an ordinary rose."

An insightful fox appears and challenges the Little Prince's perspective: "Go look at the roses again. You'll understand that yours is the only rose in all the world."

The Little Prince does, and suddenly he views his rose in a new light and returns to the bevy of other flowers in the garden. He declares, "You're nothing at all like my rose. . . . But my rose, all on her own, is more important than all of you together, since she's the one I've watered. Since she's the one I put under a glass. Since she's the one I sheltered behind a screen. Since she's the one for whom I killed the caterpillars. . . . She's *my* rose."

The fox declares, "It's the time you spent on your rose that makes your rose so important."

The Little Prince gives us insight into confirming that you've found the man or woman you want to marry. Regardless of whether you believe God has only one or many people you could spend the rest of your life with, *your* special rose is the one you choose to take care of. The Little Prince discovered this profound truth: you love who you invest in. You know you found The One when you genuinely love them, wholeheartedly commit to them, and are ready to serve them in a Christian marriage.

How Do You Know You Found "The One"?

No one should be able to talk you into getting married. Just as breaking up is always your choice, so is marriage. Each person must go through a personal journey of deciding in their own way and on their own timeframe. Relationship expert Steve Arterburn notes, "Your experience of 'knowing'—whether it's a bolt out of the blue or a gradual awareness—will be unique to you. However you reach that point, it will likely be because you find your deepest, unspoken relationship questions answered in this person."[2]

I don't know the specific questions in your heart you need to answer, but start with this foundational one: Do you genuinely love the person? Although God uses sexual attraction, passion, and emotional highs to bring people together in dating, these butterflies are not the height of love. True love is "the intention to act for the good of the object."[3] When love is intoxicating, it's not love. As dating comes to an end and marriage begins, so starts the opportunity for true love. As Gary Chapman states, "True love cannot begin until the 'in-love' experience has run its course."[4]

Likewise, desire isn't love. Desire is to "long for; crave; want."[5] Dallas Willard adds, "It cannot be said too often that agape love is not desire, and not delight. Desire and feelings generally have a different nature than love, and if we don't understand this clearly, we will remain helpless to enter into love and to receive it into ourselves."[6] True love does the opposite—it gives.

The Little Prince finally understood that he loved the rose not because of her unique beauty or his feelings toward her but because he invested in the relationship. His heart became attached to her as he shooed away insects, protected her with a glass, and watered her. The more he invested, the more he loved. He understood the biblical principle: "Where your treasure is, there your heart will be also" (Matt. 6:21).

Think about buying a particular tech stock. If you purchase only one share, you'll soon forget you own it. But if you buy one thousand shares, you'll closely watch over your asset. Every day, you'll check the financial markets, make sure the company is thriving, and follow the S&P 500 Index. Because you've spent a lot of hard-earned money, you care about your stock.

It's the same principle in a healthy marriage. As you invest in your spouse and the relationship through sacrifice, service, and encouragement, seeing their deepest hopes and dreams come to fruition, you will bond together. But it's not all work—laughing at life, taking vacations, and having sex are also fun and exciting super glue for the relationship. However, couples who stop investing start growing apart. If they continue this pattern, they will entirely divest themselves from the marriage. My mentor taught me that couples get divorced not because they're not getting what they need from the relationship, but because they stop investing in each other.

Viewing love as an investment, not just a feeling, is a good start to defining it. Similarly, love has rightly been called a "choice," a "verb," or an act of the will. But its real meaning is far more profound. Love is more than anything we do or don't do, feel or don't feel.

The Bible says, "God is love, and the one who remains in love remains in God, and God remains in him" (1 John 4:16). Love became a Person: "For God so loved the world, that He gave His only Son, so that everyone who believes in Him will not perish, but have eternal life" (John 3:16). As followers of Jesus, we learn to love as Christ did because "He first loved us" (1 John 4:19). Agape love is the "first and last word in Christian theology and ethics." It means "to love the undeserving, despite disappointment and rejection."[7]

As Dallas Willard notes, love is an overall "disposition" of the heart that wills the best for someone.

Better than feeling love is *doing* love. And better than doing love is *becoming* love—a.k.a. becoming like Christ: "I will give you a new heart, and I will put a new spirit in you. I will take out your stony, stubborn heart and give you a tender, responsive heart" (Ezek. 36:26 NLT). In marriage, it won't matter if your feelings fade for a season, that challenges arise, or that other roses surround you, because you've invested time, effort, and care into one person. You'll want to protect your relationship. True love "bears all things, believes all things, hopes all things, endures all things" (1 Cor. 13:7 ESV).

As you home in on engagement and pour your love into another, he or she needs to do the same for you. Rarely do people marry only to serve the other. You have every right to expect reciprocation of your own love and investment. As Gary Chapman notes, "Our most basic emotional need is not to fall in love but to be genuinely loved by another, to know a love that grows out of reason and choice, not instinct. I need to be loved by someone who chooses to love me, who sees in me something worth loving."[8]

You know you've found The One when you're transitioning from feelings-based love to the giving kind of love, and your partner is doing the same for you.

There Is No *Try* in Marriage

On my fortieth birthday, I wanted to learn how to do a standing backflip. I was way past the recommended age of learning gymnastics, but I had to prove to myself that, *Hey, I still got it!* After watching a few videos on YouTube, I called a parkour gym and booked an appointment for a private lesson. I arrived an hour later and was surrounded by a sea of athletic teenagers. My gangly seventeen-year-old instructor guided me to a room full of monkey-like creatures flinging themselves around metal bars and hanging on walls by their fingertips. They ran around the facility, easily flipping their bodies like a wet noodle. I was a bit intimidated.

First, my teacher performed a couple of backflips to demonstrate. Then he had me carry out several warm-up exercises, such as jumping straight up into the air while forcefully driving my knees to my chest. After that, I practiced jumping up and falling flat on my back on the mat. Thirty-five minutes later the instructor believed I was ready to try an unaided backflip.

Only two viable options presented themselves. Either I'd launch myself into success and bragging rights on social media or into the emergency room. Before I knew which, my young teacher gave me some surprising wisdom. Like a much older sage, he placed his hand on my shoulder, looked me square in the eye, and said, "The only thing I require of you is full commitment." He was profoundly correct.

Backflips require you to go all-out. *Half* backflips don't exist. There are not even 90-percent backflips. You either rotate your body 360 degrees or land on the wrong part of your body and get an expensive ride in a van with flashing lights and blaring sirens. Yoda from *Star Wars* had similar words for his padawan Luke: "Do or do not. There is no try."

Standing on the mat, I thought, *What if I jump up, stall, and freak out? What if I land on my head? What if this is my last birthday on earth?* Those were all possibilities if I *half-committed*. But I was going to do this. It was time for full commitment.

Marriage requires 100 percent commitment. You don't *try* marriage—otherwise, you might land on your head. Men and women who understand commitment and perseverance don't quit when faced with adversity. They aren't flippant. Instead, their hearts are set on working out problems and not giving up. *Divorce* is not a word found in their vocabulary. They are "in it to win it" no matter what. Put another way, they persevere—they dig in their boot heels when things get tough. It takes the grit of those like my grandparents who were married seven decades. They embrace what Paul encourages them to do: "Let us not grow weary of doing good, for in due season we will reap, if we do not give up" (Gal. 6:9 ESV). James 5:11 states, "Behold, we consider those blessed who remained steadfast" (ESV).

Something spiritual happens when we stay put. When we work through challenging storms, love grows, trust builds, joy ensues, and flowers bloom. Over time, we eat the fruit of perseverance. And only through the Lord's nutrients can we be sustained.

Like a backflip, there is no other way to be married unless you fully commit to it in faith. You have found The One when you've had a stable, committed relationship and understand what marriage will require.

With my young instructor's words firmly in my mind, I jumped up, threw my arms to the sky, looked backward, and trusted my body would rotate. Less than a second later, I had successfully spun all the way around. I completed a backflip. After two more tries, I threw my body up in the air again and landed standing up. If you want to impress a gaggle of teenagers, walk into a parkour gym when you're more than twice their age and do a backflip. If you want to impress God, learn to commit.

You Can Answer Two Important Questions

Answering two critical questions can test whether you're ready to commit to marriage. First, if you have kids, do you want your little boy or little girl to be like this future wife or husband? Your child will grow up mirroring the attitudes, beliefs, and values of you and your spouse. Everyone has idiosyncrasies, but make sure the person you choose to marry has no serious bad habit that you wouldn't want to pass on to your children. On the positive side, one of the telltale signs that you've found The One is that you look forward to your partner being your child's biggest role model one day.

The second question is more extreme. If your husband or wife ends up paralyzed, receives a cancer diagnosis, or their body or health changes significantly, would you stay married? God forbid any tragedy would occur in your family, but there are reasons to ask this theoretical question. If you can envision staying committed during a crisis like a lifelong medical condition, it shows that you love and enjoy the person. It also shows that you could have a fun, life-giving relationship, even in the face of trials.

Your Dating Relationship Has Experienced Four Seasons

The natural changes in weather from summer to autumn, to winter, and to spring compares to the regular cycle of ups and downs between couples.

Most relationships begin in "summer." Summers are exciting, carefree, affectionate periods. You and that cute guy or gal may have recently met, or you might be a committed couple who is emerging from a spring season (which will make more sense later). The sweet, emotional flowers are in full bloom, and love abounds. Acts of affection, like holding hands and kissing, flow easily in this warm and pleasant time. Frolicking to work isn't out of the question, either. Nor is singing love songs out loud in your car. The relationship is exuberant. You might continuously text this knight or princess, regularly take walks, cook together, or talk on the phone every chance you get. Overall, you enjoy every activity alongside each other. Why? Because you feel fantastic.

In autumn, ebullience levels off. Sometimes the sun shines, but the weather is also cloudy. You bicker with your partner more than you would like. Overall, you feel blasé with him or her and may not know why. Though you still experience times of enjoyment and laughter in the relationship, occasionally you feel bored, melancholy, or dissatisfied. Physical affection and intimacy still exist, but now it takes more work. In autumn, you wonder, *What happened to that easy summer love?*

In winter, your relationship turns cold and stormy. A terrible fight might have caused a serious rift. Or a calamity could have initiated this cold spell. The loss of a family member, a moral failure, or merely a lingering fall season plummeted your relationship into winter. You begin to catch yourself blaming your partner for this cold season and find it easier to focus on their faults instead of your own. Both of you are worn out. The relationship might even be in survival mode. Sometimes the thought crosses your mind, *Did I make the right choice in committing to this person?* Still, you find hope, grow closer to God, and stay faithful to your partner even though you don't feel like it. You lament as you remember how much fun you had in the summertime. You sigh and ask yourself, "Will winter be forever?"

Eventually a glowing sun parts the clouds and spring arrives. The painful remnants of winter are soothed by a warm, soothing breeze of hope. Hearts soften. Joy returns. Sentiment buds. Smiles sneak in unnoticed. You and your partner relish time together again. Lovey-dovey acts toward each other come with greater ease. As you look back, you realize how much you've learned about yourself and the other person by trudging through the arctic *together*.

Because of the cold spell, not despite it, you feel closer to your loved one, and your bond is unshakeable.

Has your relationship completed all four seasons? Though each relationship is unique, couples in long-term dating, and especially marriage, are sure to experience the summer, autumn, winter, and spring seasons in varying degrees. For dating couples, my recommendation is that you wait for marriage until you've made it through some type of winter then into spring before getting engaged. In relationship-time, that generally takes at least a calendar year. Most couples who make it through a winter season show they have staying power for the long haul.

If you date for a year or two and a trial never presents itself, life *will* guarantee one later. Still, look for signs that your mate has staying power. Solid character will show itself if your partner has overcome a personal obstacle, completed an arduous degree, or stayed faithful at a job they disliked. Sadly, some immature people try desperately to live in a never-ending summer. By doing so, these idealists (or emotionally unavailable individuals) aren't willing to embrace life's stressful times. They balk at growing up and avoid looking at their own baggage, because they can't let go of the way things *should be* in marriage. Look for a man who can endure trying times. Find a woman who can "laugh at the days to come" (Prov. 31:25 NIV).

You Understand a Christian Marriage

Do you understand that Christian marriage is a covenant—a solemn promise a man and woman make to each other before God for the entirety of their lives?[9] Timothy Keller explains: "When exchanging vows, couples are 'speaking vertically' before they speak horizontally."[10] They make this powerful promise in front of witnesses on earth and God in heaven. Couples promise "to have and to hold from this day forward, for better for worse, for richer for poorer, in sickness and in health, to love and to cherish, till death us do part."[11] You're committing to take care of your rose no matter what the emotional weather brings. Marriage is "far more durable, binding, and unconditional than one based on mere feeling and affection."[12]

As you transition from a dating mentality to a marriage one, you'll learn to actually love your partner. My mentor was adamant that keeping score in marriage must be gone, along with bargaining and an "if/then" mentality of giving and receiving love. Quid pro quo doesn't exist in a covenant marriage. God doesn't keep score, so neither should husbands and wives. Don't worry about over-giving when you're not receiving, because you'll be filled with something more profound than a spouse could ever provide.

Does this kind of marriage sound idealistic? Too difficult? The sacrificial love that comes from a covenant marriage is a risky endeavor. You wouldn't trust your emotional and physical needs to just anyone with a pretty smile or chiseled jawline. Make sure your boyfriend or girlfriend understands marriage as a covenant and wants this same foundation before you get engaged. Just because you marry in a church doesn't mean your relationship is built on Christ.

If you have been dating for a while and have a nagging doubt whether someone is the right marriage partner for you, take time, pray, and meet with a pastor or a counselor. Answer your uncertainty before you get engaged. That is why I'm a fan of *pre-engagement* counseling. Newly engaged couples reenter a summer season and often can't defog each other's rose-colored glasses to notice potential problems. So fixing the hardest issues is easier before you give or receive an engagement ring. You can work together and focus on the issues at hand while not being distracted by wedding planning.

You Found The One—Now What?

It's time to get engaged when you have assessed the relationship and know it will glorify God, bring life to you and others, and you hold a deep sense of knowing that they are The One. Planning a wedding is important, but premarital counseling is imperative. For its shortcomings, premarital counseling directly addresses topics like sex, gender roles, and past trauma that are less appropriate to discuss before engagement. I don't understand couples who "don't have time" to meet with a marriage coach in preparation for the most daunting human relationship. If you have time to plan a wedding, you have time for premarital counseling. If you don't, you're not ready to be married. It's not an elixir or a magical potion that stops all marital problems, but you'll get to know each other more, agree on how to handle finances, and set expectations on household chores.

> When you get engaged, it's *now* time to start seeing your partner through the rose-colored glasses.

The average cost of a wedding in the United States, as of this writing, is $28,000.[13] One shocking study revealed an inverse relationship between the amount of money spent on the engagement ring and the wedding ceremony to the duration of the marriage.[14] The correlation suggests that spending more before you get married increases the likelihood of divorce. Whether your ceremony is quaint or extravagant, make sure you know what matters most: investing in your relationship.

That includes continuing to engage with friends and family. Healthy engaged couples spend time with their friends and family. We all know the inseparable pair—they are the ones attached at the hip, who cut out community in favor of never-ending one-on-one time. They melt down when they're away from their soul mate for more than ten milliseconds. There's no room for Jesus between them and no room for others. Jilting community isn't good, because couples need its emotional and spiritual support now and after marriage. The adage in many countries is that it takes a village to raise a child. Likewise, communities also cultivate strong engagements and marriages.

Finally, when you get engaged, it's *now* time to start seeing your partner through the rose-colored glasses I cautioned you about before. When you decide to get married, put them on and don't take them off. Commit yourself to see all your partner's good qualities and affirm their gifts and talents. Learn to magnify your partner's positive traits and minimize his or her negative ones. Vanquish comparison. The *I-wish-she-were-more-like* or *I-hope-one-day-he-will-be-more-like* days are over. Instead, keep finding ways that you are thankful for this person. You actively overlook unimportant shortcomings because you've decided, *I'm going to love this person no matter what.*

A Fantastic Future Awaits You

When you understand God's love and how Christian marriage is different, and when you have answered the deepest questions in your heart, you're ready to enter the final stage in the romantic process—marriage. For the Christian, the best parts of love and romance are in marriage. And I'm not referring only to sex. You get to plan a life together, dream about where you want to live, build the kind of home you want to create, and maybe bring precious little lives into the world.

The Little Prince said, "People where you live [on earth] grow five thousand roses in one garden . . . yet they don't find what they're looking for. . . . And yet what they're looking for could be found in a single rose, or a little water . . ."[15] Indeed, there were thousands of other viable roses in the garden, but what made his special was that he tended to her, nurtured her, guarded her, and loved her. Your partner isn't the person who dropped out of heaven with a ray of shining light. Instead, he or she is the person you have chosen to love, serve, and stick with, whatever season of life your relationship is in.

Finding The One to marry is the goal, but just as important is how you make that decision. The way you date and what you learn as you date will prepare you for a marriage that honors God, grows you in Christ, and prepares for a loving and life-giving marriage. And whether you marry or remain single, a fantastic future awaits you, because you have prepared yourself to take wisdom with you and leave the unnecessary complications behind.

Acknowledgments

I wrote this book standing on the shoulders of relationship giants, not the least of which was my late mentor, Dr. Timothy Nelson. He taught me, counseled me, and poured his expertise and heart into me for seventeen years. Thank you, Tim. You modeled a life worth imitating, and I'll see you in heaven one day. To his wife, Dr. Jennifer Koenig Nelson, thank you for pouring your relationship knowledge into me as well.

Another heartfelt "thank you" goes to everyone on my publishing team at Moody. Amy Simpson, thank you for believing in me and this project, and for giving me my first opportunity to write a book. Ginger Kolbaba, your edits greatly strengthened my work while your encouragement inspired me. I am also grateful for Charles Snyder, a student editor, who provided feedback on the manuscript. To the cover designers Erik Peterson and Kelsey Fehlberg, your talents created an eye-catching, hilarious, and truly one-of-a-kind cover. Now I know how insightful and valuable a professional publishing team can be.

I cannot forget my many friends who became a veritable "first line of defense" against me scribing any dating heresy. Your edits, comments, and support for this book were invaluable. Specifically, I'd like to thank Dawn Garber, Lindsay Blackburn, Sarah Wheway, and Anthony Mincer.

Thank you to my mom, Joann Rose, my dad, Denny Demeter, and my stepdad, Rowland Rose, who encouraged me to "Go for it!" and cheered me on as I wrote this book. To my uncle Scott Brown, thank you for telling me years ago that if God had something to say through me then nothing would stop it.

This book began with a writing retreat in the heart of the Colorado Rockies at YWAM Cimarron. I returned a second time a year later to continue its development. Thank you to the staff who welcomed me with open arms and housed me in splendid cabins.

To Andrea Vinley Converse, Kim Washburn, and Isabelle Owens, thank you for your insights, feedback, and guidance on my book proposal.

My gratitude also goes out to my guy friends who I bantered with over countless conversations on the deck, eating three-dollar pizzas, over coffee, and during hiking and camping trips. Throughout the years, each of your friendships has made this book richer. Specifically, I'd like to thank Jeremy Slough, Sumeet Gulati, Oleg Zakusilov, Aaron Causey, William Linton, Aaron Thurston, Matt Terui, Yemi Mobolade, and Chris Russell.

There's no more prominent shoulder I relied upon than my Lord and Savior, Jesus Christ. Thank you for teaching me how much You value relationships, and with what great respect men and women should treat each other as they date. You taught me the importance that "in everything, therefore, treat people the same way you want them to treat you, for this is the Law and the Prophets" (Matt. 7:12). May this book honor You and give You glory.

Notes

Introduction: Less Pain and More Joy in Dating

1. B. J. Beitzel, "Marriage, Marriage Customs," in *Baker Encyclopedia of the Bible,* vol. 2, ed. Walter Elwell (Grand Rapids, MI: Baker Book House, 1988), 1407.

2. Henry Cloud, *How to Get a Date Worth Keeping* (Grand Rapids, MI: Zondervan, 2005), 30.

Chapter 1: Is Marriage Better than Singleness?

1. "'For I know the plans that I have for you,' declares the LORD, 'plans for prosperity and not for disaster, to give you a future and a hope'" (Jer. 29:11).

2. Richard L. Pratt Jr., *Holman New Testament Commentary: 1 & 2 Corinthians,* vol. 7 (Nashville, TN: Broadman & Holman, 2000), 114.

3. See Craig Blomberg, *Matthew,* vol. 22 (Nashville, TN: Broadman & Holman Publishers, 1992), 294.

4. John Nolland, *The Gospel of Matthew: A Commentary on the Greek Text* (Grand Rapids, MI: Eerdmans, 2005), 781.

5. Juliet Perry, Tim Hume, and Livia Borghese, "Mother Teresa Declared a Saint Before Huge Crowds in the Vatican," CNN, September 4, 2016, https://www.cnn.com/2016/09/04/europe/mother-teresa-canonization/index.html.

6. See "U.S. Marriage Rates Hit New Recorded Low," United States Congress Joint Economic Committee, April 29, 2020, https://www.jec.senate.gov/public/index.cfm/republicans/2020/4/marriage-rate-blog-test. In 2015, government data revealed that by age seventy-five, 96 percent of Americans will have been married at some point. Nathan Yau, "Percentage of People

Who Married, Given Your Age," FlowingData, December 22, 2017, https://flowingdata.com/2017/11/01/who-is-married-by-now/.

7. Robert H. Shmerling, "The Health Advantages of Marriage," Harvard Health blog, November 18, 2016, https://www.health.harvard.edu/blog/the-health-advantages-of-marriage-2016113010667.

8. Ibid.

9. Chris M. Wilson and Andrew J. Oswald, "How Does Marriage Affect Physical and Psychological Health? A Survey of the Longitudinal Evidence," IZA Discussion Paper No. 1619, May 2005, http://ftp.iza.org/dp1619.pdf.

10. "The Effects of Marriage on Health: A Synthesis of Recent Research Evidence. Research Brief," ASPE, U.S. Department of Health & Human Services, July 1, 2007, https://aspe.hhs.gov/report/effects-marriage-health-synthesis-recent-research-evidence-research-brief.

11. Shmerling, "The Health Advantages of Marriage."

12. Timothy Keller with Kathy Keller, *The Meaning of Marriage: Facing the Complexities of Commitment with the Wisdom of God* (New York: Dutton, 2011), 24.

13. W. Bradford Wilcox, "Opinion: Why Single Men May Not Be Having the Most Fun," February 13, 2016, https://www.washingtonpost.com/news/in-theory/wp/2016/02/13/why-single-men-may-not-be-having-the-most-fun/.

14. Keller with Keller, *Meaning of Marriage*, 96.

15. Linda J. Waite, Don Browning, William J. Doherty, et al., "Does Divorce Make People Happy?: Findings from a Study of Unhappy Marriages," New York: Institute for American Values, 2002, http://americanvalues.org/catalog/pdfs/does_divorce_make_people_happy.pdf.

Chapter 2: Why Is Christian Dating So Weird?

1. See *Merriam-Webster*, s.v. "awkward," accessed March 24, 2021, https://www.merriam-webster.com/dictionary/awkward.

2. Joshua Jolley, "Roland and Heidi Baker on Dating, Romance, Marriage and Covenant," October 12, 2016, http://www.joshuajolley.com/roland-and-heidi-baker-on-dating-romance-marriage-and-covenant/.

3. Dallas Willard, *Hearing God: Developing a Conversational Relationship with God* (Downers Grove, IL: InterVarsity, 1984, 1993, 1999, 2012), 34.

Chapter 3: "Scalpel, Please." Dissecting the Word *Date*

1. Henry Cloud and John Townsend, *Boundaries in Dating* (Grand Rapids, MI: Zondervan, 2000), 20.

2. Genesis 2:24 isn't writing a rule that all men will leave their families to join their wives' families. It was often the *opposite* case in the Bible. According to theologian K. A. Matthews, "It was customary in Israel for a man to remain, not leave, his father's household," as in the case of Rebekah going to live with Isaac and his family. The "leaving" that Genesis 2:24 is referring to here is metaphorical. The separation implies that the man and woman form a new emotional, psychological, physical, and spiritual bond between each other, and the man initiates this process. See K. A. Matthews, *Genesis 1–11:26*, vol. 1A, (Nashville, TN: Broadman & Holman, 1996), 223.

Chapter 4: Busting Twelve Christian Dating Myths

1. John Gottman, *The Marriage Clinic: A Scientifically-Based Marital Therapy* (New York: W.W. Norton, 1999), 18.

2. Booker T. Washington, *Up from Slavery* (Garden City, NY: Doubleday, Page & Co, 1922), 188.

3. Sheena S. Iyengar and Mark R. Lepper, "When Choice Is Demotivating: Can One Desire Too Much of a Good Thing?" *Journal of Personality and Social Psychology,* 79, no. 6 (2000): 995–1006, https://doi.org/10.1037/0022-3514.79.6.995.

4. Ibid, 995.

5. Paul W. Eastwick and Lucy L. Hunt, "So You're Not Desirable . . ." *New York Times,* May 16, 2014, https://www.nytimes.com/2014/05/18/opinion/sunday/so-youre-not-desirable.html.

6. Ibid.

7. Ibid.

8. Stacy Hubbard and The Gottman Institute, *The Seven Principles for Making Marriage Work: Singles Guide for a Better Relationship* (New York: Harmony, 2015), 34.

9. Dallas Willard, *Renovation of the Heart: Putting on the Character of Christ* (Colorado Springs, CO: NavPress, 2002), 30.

10. B. O. Banwell, "Heart," in *New Bible Dictionary*, 3rd ed., I. Howard Marshall et al., eds., (Downers Grove, IL: InterVarsity, 1996), 456.

Chapter 5: A 4,000-Pound Paper Weight: A Sturdy Frame Supports Dating

1. Gary Thomas, *The Sacred Search: What If It's Not about Who You Marry, But Why?* (Colorado Springs, CO: David C Cook, 2013), 235.

2. Mark A. Lamport, ed., *Encyclopedia of Martin Luther and the Reformation*, vol. 2 (Lanham, MD: Rowman & Littlefield, 2017), 264.

3. Dallas Willard, as quoted in Andy Peck, "Following Jesus and Living in the Kingdom," Renovaré, April 2002, https://renovare.org/articles/living-in-the-kingdom.

4. Dallas Willard, *The Divine Conspiracy* (San Francisco: HarperOne, 2014), 310.

5. Ibid.

6. I. Howard Marshall, "Disciple," in *New Bible Dictionary*, 3rd ed., I. Howard Marshall et al., eds. (Downers Grove, IL: InterVarsity, 1996), 277.

7. Henri J. M. Nouwen, Michael J. Christensen, and Rebecca Laird, *Spiritual Formation: Following the Movements of the Spirit* (San Francisco: HarperOne, 2010), 18.

8. Melissa G. Hunt, Rachel Marx, Courtney Lipson, and Jordyn Young, "No More FOMO: Limiting Social Media Decreases Loneliness and Depression," *Journal of Social and Clinical Psychology* 37, no. 10 (2018): 751–68, https://guilfordjournals.com/doi/pdf/10.1521/jscp.2018.37.10.751; Dar Meshi, Anastassia Elizarova, Andrew Bender, and Antonio Verdejo-Garcia, "Excessive Social Media Users Demonstrate Impaired Decision Making in the Iowa Gambling Task," *Journal of Behavioral Addictions* 8, no. 1 (2019): 169–73, https://doi.org/10.1556/2006.7.2018.138.

9. See Christina Camilleri, Justin T. Perry, and Stephen Sammut, "Compulsive Internet Pornography Use and Mental Health: A Cross-Sectional Study in a Sample of University Students in the United States," *Frontiers in Psychology* 11 (2020), https://www.ncbi.nlm.nih.gov/pmc/articles/PMC7835260/; Jonathan Berger et al., "Survey of Sexual Function and Pornography," *The Journal of Urology* 197, no. 4S, Supplement (May 16, 2017), https://www.auajournals.org/doi/pdf/10.1016/j.juro.2017.02.3153; Samuel L. Perry and Cyrus Schleifer, "Till Porn Do Us Part? A Longitudinal Examination of Pornography Use and Divorce," *Journal of Sex Research* 55, no. 3 (2018): 284–96, https://pubmed.ncbi.nlm.nih.gov/28497988/.

10. Timothy Keller with Kathy Keller, *The Meaning of Marriage: Facing the Complexities of Commitment with the Wisdom of God* (New York: Dutton, 2011), 21.

Chapter 6: Follow the Stages for a Great Relationship

1. "The History of the Tour de France," accessed March 12, 2021, https://www.letour.fr/en/history.

2. Colin Henrys, "Tour de France 2019 in Numbers | Can You Guess the Fastest Recorded Speed?," BikeRadar, July 30, 2019, https://www.bikeradar.com/features/tour-de-france-2019-in-numbers/.

3. William Shakespeare, *A Midsummer Night's Dream*, act 1, scene 1.

4. Robert J. Sternberg, *Duplex Theory of Love: Triangular Theory of Love and Theory of Love as a Story*, accessed March 12, 2021, http://www.robertjsternberg.com/love.

5. Song of Solomon, also known as Song of Songs.

Chapter 7: Make a List but Avoid Creating Frankenstein

1. My mentor taught that exuberant feelings in dating are like "candy." While delightful to eat, they aren't meant to sustain a relationship.

2. Henry Cloud and John Townsend, *Boundaries in Dating: How Healthy Choices Grow Healthy Relationships* (Grand Rapids, MI: Zondervan, 2000), 92.

3. William Shakespeare, *The Merchant of Venice*, act 2, scene 7.

4. Cloud and Townsend, *Boundaries in Dating*, 249.

5. Gary Thomas, *The Sacred Search: What If It's Not about Who You Marry, but Why?* (Colorado Springs, CO: David C Cook, 2013), 61.

6. Naomi Schaefer Riley, *'Til Faith Do Us Part: How Interfaith Marriage Is Transforming America* (New York: Oxford University Press, 2013), 122.

7. Ibid.

8. Ed Stetzer, "Marriage, Divorce, and the Church: What Do the Stats Say, and Can Marriage Be Happy?" *Christianity Today*, February 14, 2014, https://www.christianitytoday.com/edstetzer/2014/february/marriage-divorce-and-body-of-christ-what-do-stats-say-and-c.html. Emphasis added.

9. Charles E. Stokes, "Findings on Red and Blue Divorce Are Not Exactly Black and White," Institute for Family Studies, January 22, 2014, https://ifstudies.org/blog/findings-on-red-and-blue-divorce-are-not-exactly-black-and-white.

10. Ibid. As stated in the Stokes article, researchers are unsure why couples who have a "nominal" faith—defined as attending a religious service less than twice a month—produce a higher divorce rate. More studies are needed.

11. M. Fulwiler, "Eight Myths About Relationships," The Gottman Institute, January 21, 2015, https://www.gottman.com/blog/8-myths-about-relationships; Kirsten Gravningen, et al., "Reported Reasons for Breakdown of Marriage and Cohabitation in Britain: Findings from the Third National Survey of Sexual Attitudes and Lifestyles (Natsal-3)," *PLOS One* 12, no. 3 (March 23, 2017): e0174129, https://www.ncbi.nlm.nih.gov/pmc/articles/PMC5363851/.

12. Thomas, *The Sacred Search*, 19.

13. Neil Katz, "Life-Size Barbie's Shocking Dimensions (PHOTO): Would She Be Anorexic?" CBS News, April 21, 2011, https://www.cbsnews.com/news/life-size-barbies-shocking-dimensions-photo-would-she-be-anorexic/.

14. Andy Stanley, *The New Rules for Love, Sex, and Dating* (Grand Rapids, MI: Zondervan, 2015), 50.

Chapter 8: Unfriend-Zoning People and Other Ways to Meet Dates

1. Linda James, @kerravon, Twitter post, January 23, 2018, https://twitter.com/kerravon/status/955691460388507648

2. W. D. Reyburn and E. M. Fry, *A Handbook on Proverbs* (New York: United Bible Societies, 2000), 393.

3. W. Baker and E. E. Carpenter, *The Complete Word Study Dictionary: Old Testament* (Chattanooga, TN: AMG Publishers, 2003), 651.

4. Dallas Willard, "The Redemption of Reason," presented at the academic symposium, "The Christian University in the Next Millennium," Biola University, February 28, 1998, https://dwillard.org/articles/redemption-of-reason-the.

Chapter 9: Sex, True Purity, and Almost Jumping Out of a Moving Car

1. Craig Blomberg, *The New American Commentary: Matthew* (Nashville, TN: Broadman, 1992), 100.

2. Barry J. Beitzel "Sex, Sexuality," in *Baker Encyclopedia of the Bible*, vol. 2, ed. Walter A. Elwell (Grand Rapids, MI: Baker Book House, 1988), 1931.

3. Peter Kreeft, "Sexual Symbolism," accessed February 17, 2021, https://www.peterkreeft.com/topics-more/sexual-symbolism.htm.

4. Lawrence O. Richards, *The Teacher's Commentary* (Wheaton, IL: Victor Books, 1987), 357.

5. Spiros Zodhiates, ed. "φεύγω pheúgō," *The Complete Word Study Dictionary: New Testament* (Chattanooga, TN: AMG Publishers, 1993), 2000.

6. Paul J. Achtemeier, *Harper's Bible Dictionary,* 1st ed. (San Francisco: Harper & Row, 1985), 319.

7. Wesley L. Gerig, "Fornication," in *Baker Encyclopedia of the Bible*, 815.

8. Ben Witherington III, as quoted in Jerry Walls and Seedbed, "Is Premarital Sex a Sin? Bible Scholars Respond," Seedbed, August 7, 2012, https://www.seedbed.com/is-premarital-sex-a-sin-bible-scholars-respond.

9. Ibid.

10. Bill T. Arnold, as quoted in Jerry Walls and Seedbed, "Is Premarital Sex a Sin?"

11. Frederick J. Long, in discussion with the author, July 2020.

12. Katherine Wu, "Love, Actually: The Science behind Lust, Attraction, and Companionship," Science in the News, Harvard University, February

14, 2017, http://sitn.hms.harvard.edu/flash/2017/love-actually-science-behind-lust-attraction-companionship/.

13. Inna Schneiderman, Orna Zagoory-Sharon, James F. Leckman, et al., "Oxytocin During the Initial Stages of Romantic Attachment: Relations to Couples' Interactive Reciprocity," *Psychoneuroendocrinology*, 37(8), (2012): 1277–1285, https://doi.org/10.1016/j.psyneuen.2011.12.021.

14. "In Brief: Hugs Heartfelt in More Ways than One," Harvard Health, March 2014, https://www.health.harvard.edu/newsletter_article/In_brief_Hugs_heartfelt_in_more_ways_than_one; Bruce A. White and Susan P. Porterfield, *Endocrine and Reproductive Physiology,* 4th ed. (Philadelphia: Elsevier Mosby, 2012), 108.

15. Olga A. Wudarczyk et al., "Could Intranasal Oxytocin Be Used to Enhance Relationships?: Research Imperatives, Clinical Policy, and Ethical Considerations," *Current Opinion in Psychiatry* 26, no. 5 (2013): 474–84, https://doi.org/10.1097/yco.0b013e3283642e10.

16. Scott Edwards, "Love and the Brain," Harvard Mahoney Neuroscience Institute, accessed November 18, 2020, https://neuro.hms.harvard.edu/harvard-mahoney-neuroscience-institute/brain-newsletter/and-brain/love-and-brain.

17. Thomas Baumgartner, et al., "Oxytocin Shapes the Neural Circuitry of Trust and Trust Adaptation in Humans," *Neuron* 58, no. 4 (2008): 639–50, https://doi.org/10.1016/j.neuron.2008.04.009.

18. Hubbard and the Gottman Institute, *The Seven Principles*, 30.

19. Ibid.

20. C. S. Lewis, *Mere Christianity* (San Francisco: HarperOne, 1980), 102.

21. G. K. Chesterton, *What's Wrong with the World* (London: Cassell and Co., 1910,) 39.

22. Gerhard Kittel, ed., *Theological Dictionary of the New Testament,* vol. 2 (Grand Rapids, MI: Eerdmans, 1964), 340.

Chapter 10: Getting the Best from a Breakup

1. See "Pursuing Truth in Love" Conference, with Dallas Willard. Session One: *Discipleship and Your Cross*, recorded May 8-10, 2003, Retrieved from http://old.dwillard.org/resources/Audio/The_Cross_and_Discipleship_Part_1.mp3 on March 23, 2021.

2. See "We Are Only Challenged by Goodness Part 2," with Graham Cooke. Episode 11: The Art of Thinking Brilliantly, recorded 2011. Retrieved from http://www.brillianttv.com/videos/tatb-session4-part2.

3. Lina Kim, "Tim Keller Encourages Christians to Hold to God's Promises," Christianity Daily, April 30, 2020, http://www.christianitydaily.com/articles/9312/20200430/throughout-the-pandemic-tim-keller-reminds-christians-to-trust-gods-words-and-promises-during-difficult-times.htm.

4. Michael Rosen and Helen Oxenbury, We're Going on a Bear Hunt (New York: Little Simon, 2009).

5. Chad Brand, ed., "Forgiveness," in Holman Illustrated Bible Dictionary (Nashville, TN: Holman Reference, 2015), 589.

6. J. S. Park, "Question: The Weird Subculture of 'Christian Dating,'" J. S. Park blog, January 3, 2013, https://jspark3000.tumblr.com/post/39588152402/question-the-weird-subculture-of-christian.

7. Dallas Willard, "The Heart and It's [sic] Place in Spiritual Transformation," Podcast, Bethel University, Spiritual Renewal Conference, October 10, 2008.

Chapter 11: Fall in Love with Your Cheesecake

1. This joke originates from standup comedian Jim Gaffigan, "Catsup," track 16 on King Baby, Comedy Central Records, 2009, https://open.spotify.com/album/7noeMyoFphgaDBEaBBqwbh?highlight=spotify:track:7HyKvW6Ib9ATpvkrwV1Ij8.

2. Merriam-Webster, s.v. "compatible," accessed February 18, 2021, https://www.merriam-webster.com/dictionary/compatible.

3. Merriam-Webster, s.v. "complement," accessed February 18, 2021, https://www.merriam-webster.com/dictionary/complement.

4. G. K. Chesterton, What's Wrong with the World (London: Cassell and Co, 1910), 54.

5. Max Lucado, When God Whispers Your Name (Nashville, TN: Thomas Nelson, 1994, 1999), 44.

6. Hubbard and the Gottman Institute, The Seven Principles, 8, 29.

7. Ibid., 29.

8. Ibid., 31.

9. William Shakespeare, Two Gentlemen of Verona, act 1, scene 2.

10. Gary Chapman, The 5 Love Languages: The Secret to Love That Lasts (Chicago: Northfield Publishing, 2015).

11. See 2 Samuel 8:2, Matthew 2:11, Genesis 34:12, and Micah 1:14.

12. Take the love language assessment at https://www.5lovelanguages.com/.

13. Chapman, The 5 Love Languages, 16.

14. Hubbard and the Gottman Institute, The Seven Principles, 9.

15. Garry Poole, *The Complete Book of Questions: 1001 Conversation Starters for Any Occasion* (Grand Rapids, MI: Zondervan, 2003), 17, 123.

16. Claire M. Kamp Dush, et al., "The Intergenerational Transmission of Partnering," *PLOS One* 13, no. 11 (November 13, 2018): e0205732, https://doi .org/10.1371/journal.pone.0205732.

17. Jeff Grabmeier, "Why Your Number of Romantic Partners Mirrors Your Mother," The Ohio State University, November 13, 2018, https://news.osu .edu/why-your-number-of-romantic-partners-mirrors-your-mother.

18. Nicholas H. Wolfinger, "Trends in the Intergenerational Transmission of Divorce, *Demography*, August 1 1999, 36 (3): 415–20, https://doi .org/10.2307/2648064. Though this data is from 1999, it's a seminal meta-analysis that everyone seems to quote.

Chapter 12: You Found "The One" When You Can Love Like a Prince

1. Antoine de Saint-Exupéry, *The Little Prince* (New York: Harcourt, 1943, 1971).

2. Stephen Arterburn, *Is This the One?: Insightful Dates for Finding the Love of Your Life* (Grand Rapids, MI: Zondervan, 2012), 163.

3. Dallas Willard, Session Three: *The Gospel and Salvation*. Retrieved from http://old.dwillard.org/resources/Audio/The_Cross_and_Discipleship_ Part_3.mp3

4. Gary Chapman, *The 5 Love Languages: The Secret to Love That Lasts* (Chicago: Northfield Publishing, 2015), 33.

5. "Desire," Dictionary.com, accessed March 19, 2021, https://www.dictionary .com/browse/desire.

6. Dallas Willard, "The Nature of Agape Love," Renovaré, from "Getting Love Right, presented at American Association of Christian Counselors conference, September 15, 2007, https://renovare.org/articles/the-nature-of-agape-love.

7. Reginald E. O. White, "Love," in *Baker Encyclopedia of the Bible*, vol. 2, ed. Walter Elwell (Grand Rapids, MI: Baker Book House, 1988), 1357.

8. Chapman, *The 5 Love Languages*, 33.

9. The Bible allows for divorce in cases as described in Matthew 19:9 and 1 Corinthians 7:15.

10. Timothy Keller with Kathy Keller, *The Meaning of Marriage: Facing the Complexities of Commitment with the Wisdom of God* (New York: Dutton, 2011), 83.

11. *Book of Common Prayer* (New York: Penguin Books, 2012), 313.

12. Keller with Keller, *Meaning of Marriage*, 84.

13. "The Knot 2019 Real Weddings Study," The Knot, accessed March 19, 2021, https://www.wedinsights.com/report/the-knot-real-weddings.

14. Andrew Francis-Tan and Hugo M. Mialon, "'A Diamond Is Forever' and Other Fairy Tales: The Relationship Between Wedding expenses and Marriage Duration," SSRN, September 15, 2014, https://papers.ssrn.com/sol3/papers.cfm?abstract_id=2501480.

15. Saint-Exupery, *The Little Prince*, 71.

About the Author

Eric Demeter has taken the best of his science training, theological studies, and his own experience to become an engaging blogger and writer on faith, relationships, and culture. Specifically, he teaches on dating, healthy communication, conflict resolution, and defining your identity in Christ. He also loves engaging those outside the church to show how Christ satisfies both the heart and the mind. Eric is also passionate about what makes relationships "tick" and has used his skills as a missionary, pastor, and speaker. Eric loves to reach new believers and has taught young people across the globe, including at youth prisons, youth groups, Sunday schools, men's groups, and discipleship training courses.

From his first overseas work in Haiti to his fourth time traveling around the world, Eric has a passion to share Christ and experience other cultures. At an early age, God put on his heart to help the marginalized. As a young boy, he remembers sitting alone and crying as he watched on television starving kids in developing nations and saying to himself, "I could have been born there and they in America." Since then, he has coordinated medical mission trips in the Philippines, built homes in Haiti, delivered food bags to refugees in Greece, and blessed his local community in the States.

Currently, he works with YWAM Athens where he writes and disciples young people from the Middle East. Eric also teaches communication and conflict resolution skills to YWAM staff and missionary students.

For more information, or to book Eric as a speaker, please visit ericdemeter.com.

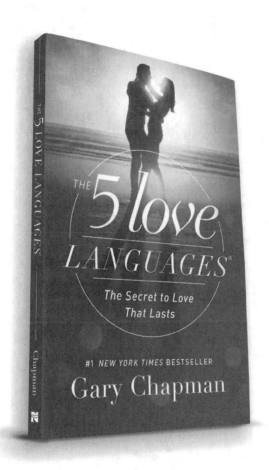

START TALKING.
AND START CONNECTING.

"Most people spend far more time in preparation for their vocation than they do in preparation for marriage."

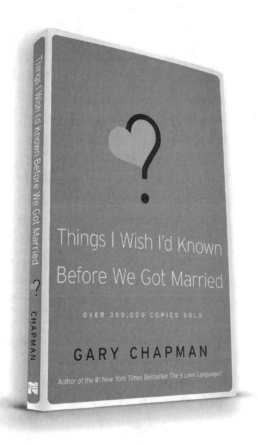